Bears, Bears and More Bears!

Written by **Gabriella Klein**
Photography by **Brad Jaeck**
and **Carol Hansen**

About the Cover

Shown on the front cover are the bears that received top prizes in the Downtown Bears It All competition. Left to right are, *Northwest Coast Bear*, created by Kristin Gjerdset, second place; *Bean E. Bear*, created by Jeff Levonian, third place; *Bizarro (the Bear)*, created by Jared Joslin, first place. All are profiled elsewhere in this book.

ISBN 0-9741541-1-3

Photographs and text
© 2004 Downtown Racine Corporation, Inc.

Graphic design by
Design Partners, Inc., Racine, Wisconsin

Created, designed and printed in the United States.

A SPECIAL TRIBUTE

    Racine lost a prominent, driving force in the community when native Racinian and SC Johnson patriarch Sam Johnson, 76, died May 22, 2004, following a battle with cancer. With his passing, Racine, Wisconsin and the world lost an outstanding businessman, a noted environmentalist and, most of all, an intense humanitarian. His impact has been felt locally and globally.

    Sam Johnson's wife Gene, the impetus behind public art in Downtown Racine, shared the fact that it was her husband who advocated for bears as this summer's artistic animal. Therefore, the 154 bears adorning our community form a special tribute to a very special person.

Table of Contents

The Enthusiasm of Many

When it was determined in the fall of 2003 that in 2004 Downtown Racine Corporation would sponsor public art for the third consecutive year, a book again was part of the plan.

This is the year for the all-out celebration. The construction projects that plagued Downtown Racine are finished. The new landscaping is done. New signs and kiosks are in place, helping direct residents and visitors alike to all Downtown Racine has to offer.

This book is part of the summer fun. It would not exist without the combined enthusiasm of many individuals and organizations – from Gene Johnson, who continues to spearhead public art in Downtown Racine, to the artists and their sponsors, and *The Journal Times*, who for the third consecutive year is helping support this Downtown fun.

Design Partners, Inc., of Racine and its very creative staff have handled the design and production of *Bears, Bears and More Bears!*, repeating their role from 2003. It's a demanding job, with lots of deadlines and pressure. They handled it superbly and I thank them for their invaluable creativity and help, and for their commitment to this book.

It's been great working with the staff at the Racine Zoo, led by President and Chief Executive Officer Jay Christie. Thanks to Marketing and Development Manager Stephanie Kratochvil for putting up with my endless questions about Andean bears and the two bears who now reside here in Racine.

As in the past two years, Brad Jaeck and Carol Hansen are responsible for the outstanding photographs. I thank them for their patience, diligence and tireless efforts. On the three books we've formed a collaboration and we've had fun while working hard. I know you'll enjoy their excellent photography as much as I do.

Special thanks to Terry Leopold of DRC. She is remarkably well-organized, an excellent proofreader, and upbeat and positive when it looks as though everything is falling apart. There's no way this book would have happened without her.

Finally, thanks to my husband Don. He is so very supportive of my projects, and he's also a great proofreader. Thanks for keeping our home together while I was out playing with bears.

– Gabriella Klein

Bears Prowl in Downtown Racine

Bears in a myriad of representations – 154 of them in all - have overtaken Downtown Racine this year, in the third consecutive summer of public art designed to attract and entertain visitors to the revitalized Downtown area. This year's event is once again sponsored by Downtown Racine Corporation (DRC) and *The Journal Times.*

The heart of public art in Downtown Racine is Imogene (Gene) Johnson, who has been vital to all three years' activities. Her idea stemmed from Chicago's *Cows on Parade* in 1999. Her thought: "If Chicago can do cows, we can do something similar."

Gene Johnson is dwarfed by Two Wrights Don't Make a Wrong *and* Berry Go Round, *the life-size bears she had commissioned by Bill Reid, to help promote this year's public art in Racine.*

In these three years, Johnson has worked closely with Cowpainters LLC, Chicago, to design the molds used to produce the fiberglass and resin animal forms that become transformed. All critters have been sized so as to attract but not intimidate.

"Mrs. Johnson was the first to insist that the animals be small enough for storefronts," said Nancy Albrecht, Cowpainters' founder. "And what a wonderful idea that was and is. We work with many small towns that are trying to lure customers back into their downtown areas and away from outlying malls," Albrecht continued, "and this is the perfect means by which to do that. Downtown Racine's projects have been an inspiration to Pinehurst, North Carolina; Deland, Florida; Lincoln, Illinois; and Helena, Montana, to name just a few," according to Albrecht. "Cowpainters is delighted to be a part of this cultural renaissance."

Why bears this year? "They have good surfaces for artists' renderings," Johnson explained, "giving the artists plenty to work with. They're friendly and inviting for artists and viewers alike."

This year's bears, all seated, are in two sizes. According to Albrecht, the bears adorned by adult artists are 29 inches high, 22 inches wide and 29 inches deep and weigh about 20 pounds. The cubs decorated by children are 20 inches high, 21 inches wide and 21 inches deep and weigh about 14 pounds. Because each bear form is individually made, sizes and weights vary slightly.

In addition, Johnson secured two life-size bears – one seated, the second standing – and had them transformed by Racine artist Bill Reid. These bears have made their home at the Downtown Racine Corporation office at 413 Main Street since early this year and are used to help promote Downtown events.

Bidding is swift and intense for the creative canines that made up Dog Days of Summer in 2002.

The unadorned bears made their initial debut in Racine October 4, 2003, at the Cat'n Around Downtown auction, proceeds of which went to support the expansion of Racine Heritage Museum and Downtown Racine activities sponsored by DRC. In 2002, the Dog Days of Summer auction proceeds were divided between the Racine Art Museum and DRC.

Patrons to The Captain's Chair are greeted by owner Paul Minneti and Hairball Pole Cat, *the artwork of Robert Andersen of Racine.*

Transforming the Bears

How were designs for the decorated bears determined? In January, artists from Wisconsin, Illinois, Minnesota, Ohio and Michigan submitted their ideas. A panel of nine reviewed more than 500 ideas from more than 400 artists and ranked each one. The 154 that received the highest scores were invited to decorate the bears.

In developing their design ideas, artists had guidelines they needed to follow. For instance, all bears must be able to endure several months on display out on the street – in all kinds of weather. So the bears needed to be durable and able to withstand all elements the outdoors offers – sun, wind, rain and dust. They also needed to be safe and durable to the public, who interacts with the decorated bruins. Above all, the designs needed to be appropriate for public display, as the entire public art event is geared toward families and children.

From early February, when artists picked up their naked bears, through April 21, when they delivered their finished works, the artists labored on their transformations. Several critters are the results of groups of people. In all, more than 200 people worked on creating the bears.

Sponsors

Each bear has its own sponsor. Businesses, organizations and individuals paid $350 to sponsor a bear. Of that, $100 went to each of the 154 lead artists to cover the cost of materials, and the remaining $250 paid for the bear sculpture.

"Sponsors are an integrally significant part of the success of public art in Downtown Racine," said Terry Leopold, DRC's special events coordinator. "Without our sponsors, we would not be able to have public art and the excitement it brings to our Downtown area."

More than 150 sponsors are involved in this summer's event.

Two-year-old Ellie Batten of Racine plays with Blue Bear Mountain Marble Maze, *created by Robert Andersen, on April 21.*

DRC staff members Terry Leopold, Devin Sutherland and Jean Garbo review the lists of bears that were delivered by their artists on April 21.

Tonya Lambeth Dilley delivers Bears of the World, *created by Dilley and her husband David, to Memorial Hall, where all the bears stayed until their first public showing May 1.*

On the Prowl

From April 21 until May 1, the bears resided in their temporary den in Downtown Racine's Memorial Hall. On May 1, they were officially on exhibit for the first time, during Bear Bash – Not Your Average Bear Affair, a fund-raising preview event.

Their public Downtown launch happened May 4, when they went on display throughout the Downtown Racine area.

They are on exhibit through the middle of September, and then are auctioned off during a public auction Saturday afternoon, September 18, at Downtown Racine's Memorial Hall. Proceeds will be used to advance DRC work and also are targeted to help fund the upgrade of Downtown's Monument Square.

Special DRC events with the bears at the center include children's Teddy Bear picnics July 20 and 21 and a book signing August 7.

Crowds and artists alike enjoy the Cat Scratch artist extravaganza and book-signing event for Cat'n Around Downtown held August 2, 2003.

(Photo by Jean Garbo)

Bears, mounted on movable platforms, wait to hit the streets of Downtown Racine May 4.

Downtown Bears It All

What should be the theme of the 2004 public-art event in Downtown Racine? That was the question facing Downtown Racine Corporation in the autumn of 2003. That is when it was decided by a DRC committee that bears would be the public-art critters of choice in 2004.

The solution? Conduct a contest to see what ideas surfaced.

"We had many great ideas – more than 650 in all – that came to us," said Devin Sutherland, executive director of DRC. "Making a final selection was a huge challenge."

In fact, three Racinians were the top prize winners, each receiving $50 gift certificates for Downtown Racine establishments. They are Joyce Lanouette, Lois Palm and Renee Popadic, who also created critters for the Dog Days of Summer in 2002 and Cat'n Around Downtown in 2003.

The winning theme – Downtown Bears It All – also brought 11 runners-up who had very close variations, according to Terry Leopold, special events coordinator for DRC. They are Karla Anderson of Madison, and Racine area residents Elwood W. Beiley, Jim Fiene, Joan Firko, Trudy George, Pauline Helman, Marion Hultman, Dianne Palmgren, Julie Pasteur, Mary Ann Schroeder and Sherry Trentadue-Forman. Each received consolation-prize gift certificates.

Why have a theme for a public-art event? "A theme helps tie everything together," said Jean Garbo, DRC's marketing director. "Our theme tells everyone the Downtown area is now finished with major construction that surrounded us in 2002 and 2003. It lets everyone know we're here and showing off what we have for people to see and enjoy."

The theme is used extensively in advertising and other promotions surrounding this year's public-art extravaganza, according to Garbo.

"People see it on billboards, in ads and brochures. They hear it on the radio. 'Downtown Bears It All' is everywhere," Sutherland said.

Artist Renee Popadic discusses one of her bears with Joyce Lanouette, left, and Lois Palm. All three were first-prize winners in the Downtown Racine Corporation bear theme competition. All are from Racine.

Downtown BEARS It All
Racine Wisconsin
SUMMER 2004

The Place to Be – Downtown Racine

After enduring more than two years of major construction projects, in 2004 Downtown Racine is enjoying the absence of road barriers, construction cones, and heavy machinery rebuilding the streets and sidewalks.

Downtown businesses and public places are welcoming residents and visitors alike. The bears add to the excitement and fun of Downtown, bordered by Lake Michigan on the east, Marquette Street on the west, the Root River on the north and Eighth Street on the south.

"This summer we're enjoying all that Downtown Racine has to offer – from unique shopping to great restaurants, many arts galleries and art-based events, lots of outdoor entertainment and fun," said Devin Sutherland, executive director of Downtown Racine Corporation. "The hardships of the past couple of years are behind us. And frankly, we're all relishing the fact that Downtown is up and running full speed. There's something here for everyone."

Emphasizing Downtown Racine's growth is the fact that in 2003 alone, more than 15 new businesses opened their doors. And more is happening this year, Sutherland said, as Downtown Racine, now a destination rather than a pass-through location, continues to be "the place to be."

Party on the Pavement, first held in October 2003 to celebrate the completion of several years of Downtown construction, is now an annual autumn event in Downtown Racine.

The Renaissance

Founded in 1848 on the shore of Lake Michigan, where the Root River meets the lake, Downtown Racine initially was the hub for this community. Conveniently located about 30 miles south of Milwaukee and 80 miles north of Chicago, the city grew into a major industrial and residential complex and Downtown Racine provided the central mercantile and social point.

In the 1960s that all changed, as Downtown Racine endured what many other industrialized cities, especially those in the Midwest, experienced – the flight outward. Downtown Racine was left with decaying storefronts, empty buildings, and

(Photo by Jean Garbo)

a general lack of interest. People turned their backs on both Lake Michigan and the Root River – except for those dedicated fishermen who came through Downtown solely to get to the water.

It was in the 1970s that things began to change, as area business people and residents took a serious look at what was happening – and envisioned what could happen with lots of planning and hard work.

Today's vibrant Downtown really started in the early 1980s. It was driven in great part by organizations and individuals who cared about the community. And by the 1990s it was obvious that a renaissance was happening.

Downtown Racine Today

Thanks in large part to a Downtown land use plan developed by Downtown Racine Corporation and adopted by Racine's City Council, Downtown Racine today bears little resemblance to the Downtown of the 1980s. It is visually attractive. It is a center for unique shops, boutiques and varied eating establishments, from quick meals to fine dining.

Perhaps one of Downtown's most exciting features is its emphasis on the arts. Sixth Street, known as Racine's Heart of the Arts, is home to many galleries and shops featuring artwork by local, regional and national artists. Racine Art Museum, opened at the corner of Fifth and Main streets in 2003, draws visitors from around the world. Internationally recognized, RAM's Karen Johnson Boyd Galleries house one of North America's most significant collections of contemporary crafts, focusing on work in ceramics, fibers, glass, metals and wood.

The Racine Heritage Museum, located on the southeast corner of Main and Seventh streets, is now planning for expanded facilities, expected to open to the public in 2005.

The Johnson Building, across Fifth Street from the Racine Art Museum, opened in 2002 and is home to Johnson Financial Group and Johnson Outdoors, as well as Carnauba Café, which draws casual daytime diners and those wanting to stop for a beverage break.

John and Peggy Griffith of Kenosha study the Racine Art Museum exhibit, The Jewelry of Robert Ebendorf: A Retrospective of Forty Years, *in the Karen Johnson Boyd Galleries from February through early May.*

Chelsie Sweeney, left, and her mother Donna of Racine, study an exhibit at the Racine Heritage Museum.

*The fountain at Splash Square is a memorial to Dr. Laurel Salton Clark, one of the astronauts
who perished in the space shuttle Columbia. Dr. Clark considered Racine her hometown.
Dedicated in the summer of 2003, enhancements to the fountain are being made in 2004.*

*Sam Johnson Parkway is a popular summer spot to relax
and enjoy music and other entertainment.*

Just south of the Johnson Building is Sam
Johnson Parkway, a wide band of open space that
stretches from Main Street east to Festival Drive. It is
here that summer concerts are held, along with many
other special events during the warm weather. It is
here that people relax on park benches and along the
landscaped walkways while enjoying Lake Michigan
to the east.

On the eastern most area of the parkway is
Splash Square. At its center is the Laurel Salton
Clark Fountain, a memorial to the astronaut who
called Racine her hometown. She died in the crash
of the space shuttle Columbia on February 1, 2003.
The fountain in her honor was dedicated in the
summer of 2003. Additions are being made to
it in 2004.

The Racine harbor and various marinas draw boaters from throughout the Midwest. Reefpoint Marina, opened in 1989, was one of the cornerstone elements in Downtown's turnaround, coupled with Festival Hall on the Lake Michigan shore.

More and more people are choosing to live in Downtown Racine, in spacious apartments and condominiums crafted in historic buildings. As retail establishments grow, people are finding Downtown gives them the goods, services and excitement they need for their daily lives.

Toward the Future

The Downtown Racine Corporation is now in the process of developing a new plan, to make sure the Downtown renaissance continues for this city of more than 81,000 people.

"We have a wonderful Downtown," Sutherland said. "We want to make sure that wonder – that specialness – continues for decades to come. We know we need to pay constant attention. With everyone working together, we can continue to build on the great strides we've made the past two decades."

Kayakers Pam and Rick Reinders of Racine enjoy the Downtown Racine skyline from the Lake Michigan perspective.

Reefpoint Marina, completed in 1989, is one of the Downtown redevelopment cornerstones.

Music is part of the scene for customers at Historic Century Market.

Over Our Head Players' theater, on Sixth Street, showcases several productions each year. Brad Kostreva, Logan Metz and Agustin Huerta, Jr., left to right, appear in Picasso of the Lapin Agile.

Lennie Farrington of the Downtown Racine Corporation staff updates information on one of the kiosks highlighting Downtown activities.

The Easter bunny greets Lauren Tuma of Racine during its April 3 visit at Crosswalk Park in Downtown Racine.

Racine artist Greg Helding takes advantage of a nice April day to paint the Monument Square area. The Johnson Building, opened in 2002, is shown on the right.

The Racine Symphony Orchestra performs both classical and summer pops concerts in the Racine area.

Andean Bears Now Reside at Racine Zoo

While Downtown Racine spent the spring of 2004 preparing for its public-art bears, the Racine Zoo, located on Main Street at Goold Street about one mile north of Downtown, was preparing for its own excitement with bears. Two Andean bears have become zoo residents. They arrived in May and have attracted a lot of attention since then.

"We're very happy to have these bears here in Racine," said Jay R. Christie, zoo president and chief executive officer. "They have adjusted very well to their new surroundings. The Racine Zoo has not had bears among its long-time residents since 1993, so this makes our new pair doubly exciting."

Andean bears are small black bears, some of whom have cream-colored circular or semi-circular markings around their eyes, which is why they are also known as spectacled bears. These light patches usually extend onto the throat and chest. They grow five to six feet long and stand two to three feet high at the shoulder. Females weigh about 150 pounds and males may reach 380 pounds or more. Their known life span is up to 35 years in captivity.

Fruit, especially berries, are a favorite food. Andean bears also eat corn, sugarcane, eggs, rodents and birds. In addition, when necessary they will consume tough plant items such as unopened palm leaves, palm nut and flower bulbs. Being agile climbers, they readily take to the trees to gather food. And yes, Andean bears enjoy honey!

Hallie finds relaxing in a hammock much to her liking.

A rare and endangered species, fewer than 2,000 Andean bears are estimated to still live in the wild. Their native continent is South America, where they are found in a wide range of habitats in Venezuela, Bolivia, Colombia, Ecuador and Peru. Most, however, are found in cloud forests, a lush, misty ecosystem of the Andes Mountains.

Currently, in the United States, only 71 Andean bears are managed by the Species Survival Plan (SSP) of the American Zoo and Aquarium Association (AZA) member institutions, among them the Racine Zoo. The SSP works closely with its

European and Russian counterparts and their 58 Andean bears to ensure future bloodlines and the survival of this species.

Both of Racine's Andean bears are part of the SSP. Diamond was born in February 1991 at the Cincinnati (Ohio) Zoo. He was on exhibit at the Smoky Mountain Zoo in Pigeon Forge, Tennessee, from March 1992 until August 2000, when he moved to the Los Angeles Zoo. At the end of 2003, he weighed in at 462 pounds, thus larger than most of his species.

When Hallie arrived in Racine, she essentially returned to her Midwestern roots. She was born in January 1986 at the Lincoln Park Zoo in Chicago. She then lived at the Sedgwick County Zoo in Wichita, Kansas, from 1992 until this spring. When she arrived in Racine, she tipped the scale at 257 pounds.

The pair is residing in temporary quarters at the Racine Zoo while their new habitat is under construction at the southeast end of the zoo. They move to their new quarters late in spring 2005.

Under the direction of the Species Survival Plan, Christie said he hopes a breeding program will be established here.

AZA member institutions, including the Racine Zoo, partner with zoos and similar conservation organizations in South America to help protect Andean bears in the wild, Christie said, "where it matters most. The continued destruction of Andean bears' habitat and hunting are the two biggest threats to the survival of this rare animal," he continued. "The Racine Zoo hopes that our Andean bear residents will assist us as we educate the public about these bears and the importance of celebrating and saving wildlife and wild places."

Special Racine Zoo Events

Racine Zoo Bear Week, commemorating the pair's arrival, was held in May, according to Stephanie Kratochvil, marketing and development manager for the zoo. In addition to daily animal chats with the animal care specialists, other activities taking place during the summer, she said, include special conservation education programs about bears. Many of the zoo's regular summer events will have a bear theme including Zoovies, the Classic Car Show, and the zoo's black tie gala, Zoo Debut.

Diamond is naturally curious and poses for his portrait.

Juliet Paradowski, curator of conservation and animal welfare, and Jay Christie, zoo president and chief executive officer, discuss plans for the new habitat for Diamond and Hallie, the Andean bears now residing at the zoo. The pair will move into their new quarters in 2005.

The Bear Family

Several species of bears make up the bear family, according to Christie.

The grizzly, or brown, bear is found chiefly in forests in northwest North America, the Scandinavian countries east to Russia, and from Syria to the Himalayas. Its size is variable, depending on its location and nutrition. Females can range from 175 to 450 pounds, males 20 to 30 percent heavier. The largest recorded grizzly – in Alaska – weighed in at 937 pounds. From the head to the tail tip they measure up to nine feet with shoulder height about four to five feet. Their coat is long and coarse, usually brown and frequently white-tipped or grizzled.

As its name indicates, the polar bear is found in the polar area of the northern hemisphere. The largest of the bear family, its body length goes up to nearly 10 feet in males, with females somewhat smaller. The highest recorded polar bear weight is 1,430 pounds.

Up to 18 subspecies exist of the American black bear, based on where they live. They're found in Northern Mexico and California north to Alaska and across the continent to the Great Lakes, then east to Newfoundland and the Appalachian mountains. Isolated populations include those in northern Florida and the north Gulf coast. They inhabit forests, wetlands and woodlands. Adult females range up to 265 pounds and males are 10 to 50 percent heavier. They measure up to nearly six feet from head to tail and up to about three feet at the shoulder. Coat color on this bear can be white, bluish, brown and black.

Other bruins, Christie said, include the sloth bear, sun bear, Asiatic black bear and the giant panda. The sloth bear is found in East India and Sri Lanka, the sun bear in Southeast Asia, the Asiatic black bear from Iran to Japan, and the giant panda in Southwest and South Central China.

The koala is not a member of the bear family. It is a marsupial, along with the likes of the opossum and kangaroo.

Tropical Ande, among the bears on display in Downtown Racine, helps call attention to the new bears at the Racine Zoo.

Tropical Ande

In honor of the new Racine Zoo inhabitants, a public-art bear, *Tropical Ande*, is part of the Downtown Racine exhibit. Sponsored by Karen and Laurel Sutherland, *Tropical Ande* was created by Racine artist Lyle Peters, who was assisted by Nathan and Quentin Sauvage of Racine, both students at The Prairie School. Peters is a retired Case High School art teacher. He received his bachelor of science degree from Western Michigan University in Kalamazoo and his master's degree from the University of Wisconsin-Milwaukee. For 25 years he was a stoneware potter. He now has returned to painting in watercolors and pastels. He is a member of the Racine Art Guild and the Wisconsin Watercolor Society.

Kids' Cubs Showcase Young Artists

When design ideas for this year's public-art event came in, it was obvious several children wanted to get into the picture.

"In the past, we've had a few entries from children younger than 13, but this year those numbers grew," said Terry Leopold, special events coordinator for Downtown Racine Corporation. Thus kids' cubs were born.

"We had the cub mold, and it seemed like the logical thing to do," Leopold explained. She said the children's design proposals were judged by the same panel of nine who reviewed the full-size-bear ideas, and 10 kids' cubs were selected.

One of the artists is 12-year-old Alex Hintz of Franksville. He and his entire family – parents Dan and Ginny and seven-year-old sister Maddie – fell in love with the dogs in 2002 "and we spent a lot of time Downtown. We were surprised every time we saw a new one," according to Alex.

Last year he submitted a design idea for a cat – adorned with Sponge Bob characters – but because no young-artists' category was available, his idea was rejected.

The third year of public art in Downtown Racine is a charm for Alex, a sixth-grader in the Wisconsin Connections Academy, a school-at-home program based in Appleton. His *Cartoon Cub* is one of the 10 cubs.

Why cartoons? "Because that's what I draw the best," Alex explained. A cartoon wall in the family's basement is a testament to Alex's creativity. It is covered with 28 cartoon characters in various stages of completion. Alex has been working on the wall for more than a year.

"In some ways, working on the bear cub is easier because the paint doesn't sink in like it does on the wall," Alex said. "But working in three dimensions is hard because I have the curves on the bear's body."

The family kitchen is turned into a studio for Alex Hintz, as he paints cartoon characters on his bear, Cartoon Cub.

Creating three-dimensional work for public-art events seems to run in the Bloom family. Last year, Rebecca Bissi-Bloom designed a cat for Racine's Cat'n Around Downtown.

This year her daughters – 12-year-old Rachel and 10-year-old Sarah – created cubs of their own, while their mom worked on her adult bear. Dad Joshua and Baby, the family's pup, provided plenty of support.

Both girls are into art of all kinds, and the Bloom home has much of it on display, from creative sculptures to wall hangings. The entire basement is a studio filled with supplies supporting the creative bent – paints, brushes, clay, dress forms, wire mesh – everything imaginable.

The laundry room has been turned into a workroom for the girls to structure their bears. Sarah, who is in the fifth grade at The Prairie School, works on the wire frame for *Bear Accessories*, while Rachel, in eighth grade at The Prairie School, works on building out *The Bear Necessities'* face and cheeks so they will be fuller.

"We like the way the two bears go together," Sarah explained. "Mine has lots of jewelry and goes with Rachel's bear."

According to Rachel, her bear is something of a play on words and is loaded with everything, hardly the "bare" necessities of life.

The biggest challenges creating their bears? "Having the time is a real problem," said Rachel, while Sarah said the "wire frame is the hardest part."

Both girls enjoy showing visitors the works they have created through the years. They are eager to explain how they are creating their bears, but they also share the fact they like to draw and sculpt. Both also are musicians, Rachel on piano and Sarah on classical guitar.

Meet the 10 Kids' Cubs

Following are the kids' cubs created for this year's Downtown Racine public-art event.

Sarah (left) and Rachel Bloom use Stonex to build out the faces on their bears, Bear Accessories *and* The Bear Necessities, *in the family's laundry room turned into an artists' studio.*

The 11 children who created kids' cubs pose with their bears when delivering them April 21. Kneeling, left to right, are Sam Carbajal, Alex Hintz, Bjørn Norderhaug, Madison McLain, Sarah Bloom and Rachel and Sarah Pettit. Standing are Mason Swager, Rachel Bloom, Kailey Lietzke and Randi Meinert.

Bear Accessories

. . . all dressed up.

Artist: Sarah Bloom, Racine

Sarah Bloom is 10 years old and is in the fifth grade at The Prairie School. She plays the classical guitar and enjoys making clay sculptures and drawing. Her dream in life is to help the poor and help her mother create a business in dogs' clothes.

Sponsor: SC Johnson

The Bear Necessities

. . .she's loaded with everything imaginable.

Artist: Rachel Bloom, Racine

Rachel Faye Bloom is 12 years old and is in the eighth grade at The Prairie School. She plays the piano and has appeared in Racine Theatre Guild productions of *Oliver!* and *A Christmas Story*. She likes to draw, sketch, paint and play "The Sims" computer game.

Sponsor: Young Rembrandts-A Children's Drawing Program

Bearitone

. . . baritone notes highlight this musical bear.

Artist: Randi Meinert, Fort Atkinson, Wisconsin

Randi Meinert is 12 years old and in seventh grade at Fort Atkinson Middle School. She plays the piano and flute. She's no stranger to public art, as she was one of the fifth graders who created Stephen Bull Dog in 2002, for Dog Days of Summer in Racine. She also helped her mother, Krista Lea Meinert Edquist, create a dog for that event.

Sponsor: Johnson Financial Group

Beary Smart

. . . mathematical and scientific equations abound.

Artist: Sam Carbajal, Racine

Sam Carbajal is an eighth grader at the R.E.A.L School. This 12-year old received a first place and an honorable mention in the Racine Literacy Council art contest in 2003. His favorite subjects are math and science. He plays the saxophone in the school band and the Junior Lighthouse Brigade. He plans to be a zoo veterinarian when he grows up.

Sponsor: The Wackenhut Corporation

Border

. . . appealing to both Green Bay Packers and Chicago Bears fans.

Artist: Kailey M. Lietzke, Racine

An honor roll sixth grader at Trinity Lutheran School, Kailey Lietzke is 11 years old. Her favorite subjects are art and math. She also enjoys reading, archery, bowling, playing her clarinet, listening and singing to country music, and playing video games. She has played in a softball league since kindergarten and also is in a volleyball league. She wants to become an artist.

Sponsors: Mark Eickhorst and Andy Spores/WRJN

Bumble Bee Bear

. . . masquerading as a bee to get to the honey.

Artist: Mason Swager, Racine

Mason Swager, 12, a seventh grader at The Prairie School, Racine, is an aspiring illustrator. He has created his own comic strip, with plans to put it on his Website. In addition to illustrating comics, Mason has played the piano since the age of seven and also plays the trumpet. His favorite sport is soccer. He will play on the Prairie 7/8 soccer team and the Prairie basketball team.

Sponsor: Crandall Arambula PC

Cartoon Cub

. . . adorned with cartoon bears.

Artist: Alex Hintz, Franksville, Wisconsin
Alex Hintz is 12 and a sixth grader at the Wisconsin Connections Academy. He enjoys drawing and welcomed the challenge of creating a bear. He plays guitar and piano. He has played basketball for Racine Youth Sports for eight years. He is actively involved in the children's ministries at Grace Church.

Sponsor: Johnson Polymer

Norwegian Nobel Peace Prize Bear

. . . depicts the annual Nobel Peace Prize awarded each October.

Artist: Bjørn Norderhaug, Brookfield, Wisconsin
Bjørn Norderhaug is a nine-year-old fourth grader at Brookfield Academy. He enjoys celebrating his Norwegian heritage by Nordic cross country skiing, sailing, and attending Skogfjordon Norwegian Language Village each summer. He recently was awarded first place for his creative writing story in Beartastic Celebration, sponsored by the Waukesha County Historical Society and Museum.

Sponsors: Michael and Linda Norderhaug

Ready to Hi-bear-nate!

. . . gathering everything needed for a long winter hibernation.

Artists: Rachel and Sarah Pettit, Racine

Rachel Pettit, 12 and in seventh grade, and Sarah Pettit, nine and in fifth grade, are students at St. Edward's School, Racine. Both are interested in art and have taken a number of art classes. Rachel plays the piano, is a St. Edward's cheerleader and has participated in several academic competitions. Sarah plays violin and soccer, and is a low green belt in tae kwon do.

Sponsor: Molly MaGruder

Smokey the Bear

. . . helping prevent forest fires.

Artist: Madison McLain, Racine

Madison McLain is 10 years old and in fifth grade at Kenosha Christian Life School. Her favorite subjects are math, science and art. Her favorite sports are volleyball, basketball and soccer. She enjoys all aspects of artwork as well as listening to music, dancing, reading, singing and playing sports. She's keeping her career options open; she'd like to be an artist, a singer, a scientist or a teacher.

Sponsors: Jean Garbo and Terry Leopold

Around Town

*These eight bears take us around
Racine – from the lakefront
to the neighborhoods.*

After the Reign of Cats and Dogs

. . . Ursa Minor finds the crowns of the cats and dogs at his doorstep; their Racine reign is over.

Artist: Bill Reid, Racine

Bill Reid does much of his work at The Prairie School in Racine, where he is artist-in-residence. He has art degrees from the Kansas City Art Institute in Kansas City, Missouri, and Cranbrook Academy of Art in Bloomfield Hills, Michigan. He shows his works around the country and hopes to have a Website in 2004. He participated in Dog Days of Summer and Cat'n Around Downtown.

Sponsor: Sam and Gene Johnson

Bearzan

. . . a tribute to the Andean bears now living at the Racine Zoo.

Artist: Brenda (Running) Stephan, Racine

Brenda Stephan is an art teacher in the Waterford Graded School District. She earned her master of education degree in educational computing from Cardinal Stritch University, Milwaukee, and her bachelor of science in art education from the University of Wisconsin-Whitewater. Her medium of choice is anything that allows her to use her hands as the primary tool. Her current creative outlet has been remodeling the home she shares with husband Bill and dog Scully.

Sponsor: Racine Zoological Society

Cub-adore of Racine

. . . keeps an eye on the shore of Racine.

Artist: Linda M. Silvasi-Kelly, Baileys Harbor, Wisconsin

A Racine native who took childhood classes at Wustum Museum of Fine Arts, Linda Silvasi-Kelly has her bachelor of fine arts degree from the University of Wisconsin-Green Bay. A freelance artist, she has illustrated several books, designed ads, logos and brochures; does faux painting, trompe l'oeil, stenciling; hand-paints furniture and walls; and designs jewelry. She participated in Dog Days of Summer and Cat'n Around Downtown.

Sponsor: Skipper Bud's Reefpoint Marina

Good, Bearable and Ugly

. . . represents the choices we have to achieve a sustainable world.

Artists: Sr. Janet Weyker and Quota Friends, Racine

Educated at St. Catherine's High School and Dominican College in Racine, Sr. Janet Weyker earned a master's degree in art education at the University of Wisconsin-Madison and studied calligraphy in Italy and England. She taught elementary and college art classes and does freelance calligraphy and design. Quota friends are Teri Jacobson, Susan Liedel and Susan Ramagli. Sr. Weyker participated in Dog Days of Summer and Cat'n Around Downtown.

Sponsor: Quota International of Kenosha-Racine

Old Glory Bear

. . . a tribute to the American flag.

Artists: Lou Ann Urness and Jim Beaugrand, Racine

Lou Ann Urness and Jim Beaugrand have more than 20 years of experience in the arts and crafts area. Urness owns Ceramic Gardens. Beaugrand, one of her students, has learned many techniques. They share a joint love of patriotic things and helping the community. They also volunteer to educate the children at Red Apple School about ceramics.

Sponsor: Studio 75 Aveda Salon and Day Spa

Pandemonium: 4th of July in Racine

. . . panda showing the fun in Racine during this summer celebration.

Artist: Julie Trafton, Milwaukee

Julie Trafton, an art specialist at North Park Elementary School, Racine, received her art education degree and master's degree in art therapy from Mount Mary College, Milwaukee. She is involved annually with the Wisconsin Art Education Association Regional Youth Art Month show. She also enjoys drawing, quilting and weaving. She participated in Cat'n Around Downtown.

Sponsor: Britton Road Press

33

Racine Bumble Bear

. . . let's see if this special Racine bear will really fly!

Artist: Bill Reid, Racine

Bill Reid, artist-in-residence at The Prairie School in Racine, works in steel, using an oxy-acetylene torch. He has been using these materials in his work for about 20 years and has made one art car of steel and is starting another one. He has certification in pressure vessel welding from the Tulsa Welding School in Tulsa, Oklahoma. He participated in Dog Days of Summer and Cat'n Around Downtown.

Sponsor: Schorsch Management/Green Bay Meadows Apartments

Romare Bearden on Our Block

. . . based on Bearden's view of New York City, but this time it's Racine

Artist: Georgette Hardy Edwards, Racine

Georgette Hardy Edwards teaches art at William Horlick High School and is art coordinator for the Racine Unified School District. She attended University of Wisconsin-Whitewater, where she earned a bachelor of science degree and a master's degree in art education. Her primary medium is ceramics. She participated in Dog Days of Summer.

Sponsor: Landmark Title of Racine, Inc.

Famous Forebears

*Historic icons come from
all walks of life – writers, explorers,
scientists and more – as shown with
these eight bears.*

Al-beart Einstein

. . . a tribute to the genius.

Artist: Melissa Rogalla, Chicago

MENSA member Melissa Rogalla, an Illinois artisan since 2000, has been working with the native arts for more than 15 years. She enjoys working in a variety of artistic media and has donated animal-themed artwork to the Anti-Cruelty Society and Treehouse Animal Foundation. She has three education degrees and currently teaches in Chicago. She has long admired Einstein and everything that is intelligent and creative.

Sponsor: Adecco

Bear-ilyn Monroe (Diamonds Are a Bear's Best Friend)

. . . dressed in a hot pink gown from movie fame.

Artists: Melissa Rogalla, Chicago, and Mike Indovina, Orland Park, Illinois

Melissa Rogalla, an Illinois artisan from the south side of Chicago, believes that her two bear designs reflect the two sides of her personality. She currently has works at the James R. Thompson Center in Downtown Chicago. Graphic artist Mike Indovina creates the ongoing graphic novel *Satyr*, which retells Greek and Roman mythology in a humorous manner.

Sponsor: The Kiefer Family

Beary Garcia

. . . in memory of the most famous Dead Head of all.

Artists: Uncle John's Band: Jennifer Andert, Pete Conti, Amanda Heinzelman, Steven Kreines, Shelley Kutis, Jeanne Peterson, Lori Peterson and Tom Yagelski, Racine; Dan Miller and Joni Miller, Caledonia, Wisconsin; Jan Willette and Jennifer Willette, Franklin, Wisconsin; and Jennifer Ruckert, Milwaukee.
Uncle John's Band is comprised of a band of data crunchers from SC Johnson and AC Nielsen, who couldn't bear to let a week fly by without a few visits Downtown to paw the pavement in and out of their favorite shops and restaurants. They participated in Cat'n Around Downtown.

Sponsor: GFWC Junior Women's Club of Racine

Li-bear-ace

. . . quite the flamboyant performer.

Artists: Cindy Sackmann and Joslyn Sackmann, Milwaukee

This mother-daughter duo is well-based in art. Mother Cindy holds a bachelor's degree in art education and commercial art from University of Wisconsin-Milwaukee; daughter Joslyn is a recent graduate of Minnesota State University, Mankato. Cindy is an art teacher in the Milwaukee Public Schools and also worked in the commercial art industry. Joslyn is talented in computer art and scrapbooking.

Sponsor: Sebastian's Fine Food and Spirits

The Red Bearon

. . . watch the sky for his prowess.

Artist: Trudi Theisen, Monona, Wisconsin

A Wisconsin native and first generation American of Swiss heritage, Trudi Theisen graduated from the University of Wisconsin-Madison with a degree in education. She has participated in numerous juried exhibitions throughout Wisconsin, Wyoming and Arizona. Her work has received many awards. She participated in Dog Days of Summer and Cat'n Around Downtown.

Sponsor: North Shore Bank

Robert "Beary" – Polar Explorer

. . . tribute to U.S. Adm. Robert Peary and partner Matthew Henson, who reached the North Pole on April 6, 1909.

Artist: Jerry E. Treiber, Racine

Jerry Treiber, a lifelong Racine resident, is the graphics manager at Quick Cable Corporation in Racine. Since 1973, he has built 52 floats for Racine's 4th of July parade. Treiber's interest in Racine history fueled the idea for this bear. William Horlick invented and produced Horlick Malted Milk in Racine and sponsored Peary's expedition with several tons of Horlick's. Photos show Peary and Henson sitting on empty boxes of Horlick's.

Sponsor: Alloc, Inc.

Teddy Bear (the original)
Teddy Roosevelt

. . . photos in his pockets show some of his accomplishments.

Artist: Jerry E. Treiber, Racine

Jerry Treiber is the graphics manager at Quick Cable Corporation. He is a designer and draftsman with two design degrees. His floats in Racine's July 4th parade have always placed in the top three. A Racine history buff, Treiber points out it was President Roosevelt who gave Robert Peary leave from the Navy to explore the polar region, leading to the discovery of the North Pole.

Sponsor: Donald and Gabriella Klein

William Shakesbeare – A Midsummer Night's Dream

. . . depicting the Bard himself and his delightful tale.

Artist: Theresa Schiffer, Racine

A graduate of the University of Wisconsin-Parkside with a major in fine art, Theresa Schiffer currently works as a feature page designer for the *Milwaukee Journal Sentinel*. Prior to that, she was the design editor for *The Journal Times*, Racine. She has won numerous state and international design and illustration awards during her career in newspapers. She participated in Cat'n Around Downtown.

Sponsor: *Milwaukee Journal Sentinel*

Fashionably Adorned

Fashion comes in many forms – from the simple to the elaborate and even whimsical. These 18 bears illustrate very different perspectives on fashion – some even appropriate for a game of marbles or just chilling out.

Baloo

. . . the blue bear struts his stuff in just the bare necessities.

Artist: Kate Proeber, Caledonia, Wisconsin

Kate Proeber, a University of Wisconsin-Parkside graduate and native Racinian, has been teaching art at Shoreland Lutheran High School in Somers, Wisconsin, since 1986. She is a member and current president of the Racine Art Guild. Her work has been shown at Charles A. Wustum Museum of Fine Arts in Racine, Anderson Gallery in Kenosha and Rotary Gardens in Janesville. She participated in Cat'n Around Downtown.

Sponsor: Plumb Gold Ltd.

Baron Prince

. . . a mythical bear of elegant nobility.

Artist: J. S. Adams, Racine

A lifelong Racine resident and mixed-media artist, James Adams also has a strong interest in digital fine art. He received his art education at Layton School of Art in Milwaukee, and is a member of Racine Art Guild, Racine Art Museum and Wisconsin Painters and Sculptors. He created *Dog Gone Wright* for Dog Days of Summer and *Copycat* for Cat'n Around Downtown.

Sponsor: Robert W. Baird & Co.

Bean E. Bear

. . . covered in mosaic stylings from design-producing beans.

Artist: Jeff Levonian, Racine

Jeff Levonian graduated from University of Wisconsin-Parkside with a bachelor of arts degree in art. He currently manages Speedtech International, Inc., and also enjoys coaching soccer at William Horlick High School. He participated in both Dog Days of Summer and Cat'n Around Downtown and paints and sculpts to relieve the stress of everyday life.

Sponsor: Dimples Fine Imports

Bear in a Blanket

. . . images showing interconnections over time.

Artist: Ada M. James, Racine

A graduate of the University of Northern Colorado, Ada James had private shows in Colorado, Wyoming and Winnetka, Illinois. Her work has been published in journals, magazines, advertising and promotional pieces. In 1998, she completed a drawing commissioned by the National Spiritual Assembly of the Baha'is of the United States on the theme of Women and Peace, included in a traveling European show. She participated in Dog Days of Summer.

Sponsor: Carpetland, USA

Bear Naked

. . . the barber must have goofed!

Artist: Teresa M. Meyers, Kenosha, Wisconsin
Born and raised in Racine County, Teresa Meyers, who works at Porters of Racine, has loved art since childhood. She expresses this through drawing, theater and, now, public art. She hand-draws her own Christmas cards and for other occasions, cards are done on request. She participated in Cat'n Around Downtown.

Sponsor: Porters of Racine

Bear Patch

. . . a very crazy quilt.

Artist: Sybil Brauneis Klug, Lake Geneva, Wisconsin
Fontana Elementary School teacher Sybil Brauneis Klug works in acrylics and oils. Color is the primary focus of her landscapes, flowers and still-life arrangements. Her paintings have been included in juried shows at the Charles A. Wustum Museum of Fine Arts, Anderson Arts Center in Kenosha and Rotary Gardens in Janesville. She participated in Dog Days of Summer and Cat'n Around Downtown.

Sponsor: All Saints Medical Group Employees, 1 Main

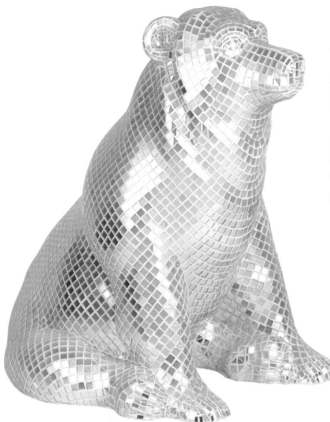

Bearly There

. . . reflecting his surroundings and blending into the background.

Artists: Karen Johnson, Jill Sturino and Darlene Heiden, Racine
Karen Johnson is the owner of Aha! Studios, an animation studio specializing in animation for computer games, toys and scoreboards. Jill Sturino is an executive assistant at SC Johnson; this is her first artistic endeavor. Darlene Heiden is a purchasing assistant at Kranz, Inc., and has been a quilter for the past 20 years. They used 5,000 mirror tiles on their bear.

Sponsor: Accents on Main

Bronze Bear

. . . elegantly coated in rich bronze.

Artists: Michael and Vernay Mueller, Racine
Vernay Mueller, a freelance artist, and Michael Mueller, a pipe layer, are native Racinians and avid collectors of antiques and Racine memorabilia. Vernay's works include two- and three-dimensional art pieces as well as decorative furniture and wall finishes. Michael's interests include photography, softball and playing Santa. They participated in Cat'n Around Downtown.

Sponsor: Knuteson, Powers and Wheeler, S.C.

Burbeary

. . . wearing the nostalgic Burberry plaid.

Artists: Robin L. Zimmerman and Carrie Nolden, Racine

Burbeary is the collaborative effort of friends who recently entered the world of parenthood. Robin Zimmerman graduated from the University of Wisconsin-Milwaukee and works as an obstetrics nurse at Kenosha Hospital. Carrie Nolden completed her undergraduate degree at the University of Wisconsin-Madison. Prior to motherhood, she was a social worker and is a certified teacher. Both enjoy Downtown Racine as a family place and as a fun evening-tme destination.

Sponsor: Racine Optical Co., Family Vision Care

Cool Blue Bear

. . . calm yet elegant.

Artist: Deb Bartelt, Oshkosh, Wisconsin

Deb Bartelt has been an elementary art teacher in the Oshkosh Area School District since 1973. She earned her bachelor's degree in art education at the University of Wisconsin-Oshkosh and her master's degree in adaptive art education from St. Norbert College, DePere, Wisconsin. Her special skills include watercolors, paper making and sketch journals. She participated in Dog Days of Summer and Cat'n Around Downtown.

Sponsor: Sandra Young

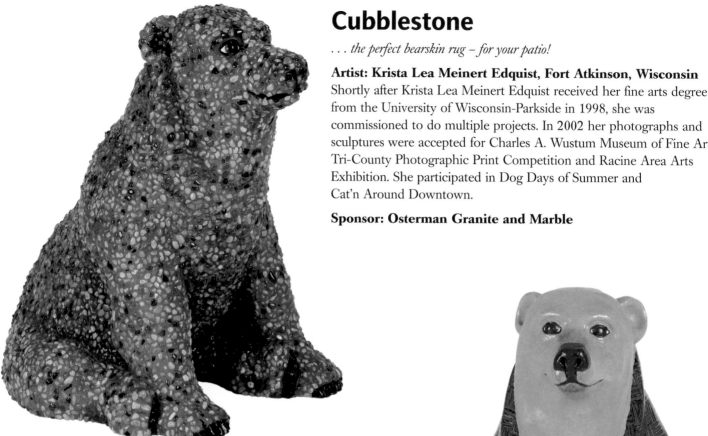

Cubblestone

. . . the perfect bearskin rug – for your patio!

Artist: Krista Lea Meinert Edquist, Fort Atkinson, Wisconsin

Shortly after Krista Lea Meinert Edquist received her fine arts degree from the University of Wisconsin-Parkside in 1998, she was commissioned to do multiple projects. In 2002 her photographs and sculptures were accepted for Charles A. Wustum Museum of Fine Arts' Tri-County Photographic Print Competition and Racine Area Arts Exhibition. She participated in Dog Days of Summer and Cat'n Around Downtown.

Sponsor: Osterman Granite and Marble

Like My Coat? Wove It Myself, Log Cabin Pattern

. . . wearing his creativity.

Artist: MaeCarol Matousek, Brookfield, Wisconsin

Inspired by a visit to the Racine Art Museum in Downtown Racine, MaeCarol Matousek designed this bear to reflect her interest in weaving. As a member of local and national weaving guilds for 30 years, she has exhibited and won awards for her work. Volunteering at Gaenslen School in Milwaukee, she enjoys sharing her love of weaving and other fiber arts. Other interests include photography and painting.

Sponsor: Racine Area Manufacturers and Commerce

Lost My Marbles

. . . looks like it was carved out of white veined marble.

Artist: Susan Gaertig, Racine

Susan Gaertig and her family have lived in Racine for six years, where she has a painting business, Decorative Painting by Susan. In her Chicago art classes, she has learned how to create beautiful wall finishes in addition to fun things like painted marble and unusual furniture pieces. Her work is found in many homes and businesses in the area.

Sponsor: Ruud Lighting, Inc.

Ms. Beary Beautiful

. . . colorful, bright and lots of sparkle.

Artist: Marilyn C. Benson, Racine

A Racine native, Marilyn Benson enjoys working in a variety of media. She is a freelance artist, graphic designer and writer, and her hobby is photography. Currently she is employed as the editor/layout designer of the *Gateway Gazette* for Gateway Technical College. She also serves on the board of directors of Countryside Humane Society and participated in Cat'n Around Downtown.

Sponsor: Lakeview Pharmacy

Polar Ice

. . . mosaic look with a cooling blue effect.

Artists: Becky Manteufel and Mike Nelson, Sturtevant, Wisconsin
Becky Manteufel currently majors in art education at the University of Wisconsin-Milwaukee. She worked as a photographer for Racine's Main Gallery program and currently has an art piece in the Union Gallery at UWM. Mike Nelson plans to attend Milwaukee Area Technical College to pursue a computer degree. Both are aspiring photographers.

Sponsor: Yamaha Motor Corporation

Quilting "B"

. . . colorful patches attract the bee.

Artists: Carey Garcia and Ingrid Wiggins, Racine
Carey Garcia, a freelance artist originally from Minnesota's Twin Cities, is a district manager with *The Journal Times*. A graduate of the University of St. Thomas, she works with acrylics, pencil, photography and sculpture. Ingrid Wiggins, a graduate of University of Wisconsin-Parkside, is president and master designer of Rare Loom Designs. She specializes in multi-texture scarves and shawls, designer jewelry and other accessories.

Sponsor: *The Journal Times*

Quilty

. . . quilted coat shows the fun this black bear has living in Downtown Racine.

Artist: Nita Showers, Burlington, Wisconsin

Primarily self-taught and using oil as her medium, Nita Showers has been painting the Teddys and Toys calendar and greeting cards for Lang Graphics for 20 years. Her work can be seen in a children's book, puzzles, needlework kits, Christmas ornaments, many paper products, on Easter eggs at the White House, in a toy museum and in a book of her bears published in Japanese.

Sponsor: Bonnie and Thomas Prochaska

Um-bear-lla

. . . holds the umbrellas ready for spring showers.

Artists: Chris and Shawn Niemiec, Racine

Chris and Shawn Niemiec, both native Racinians, have been married for eight years. Chris is a tool and die maker and Shawn a product manager. Though photography is their preferred art, they have tried their hands at woodcarving, ceramics and painting, admittedly with varying results. Their combined skills contribute to the look and utilization of their bear.

Sponsor: Maresh-Meredith and Acklam Funeral Home

Food Fanciers

These 10 bears concentrate on gastronomic delights, enjoying a picnic, desserts, outdoor cooking – and honey, of course.

All-American Bear-B-Q

. . . all set to get to work.

Artist: Julie J. Wynstra, Racine

A lifelong Racine resident, Julie Wynstra attended the University of Wisconsin-Milwaukee. She credits her creativity to her heredity. Wynstra, who works at Gardtec, Inc., is self-taught in the creative arts and enjoys sewing, knitting and crocheting. She once designed a restaurant interior to look like the Flintstone home in Bedrock, and also taught ballet classes and designed the children's costumes. She participated in Cat'n Around Downtown.

Sponsor: Gardtec, Inc.

Bear-B-Q

. . . this "Web-bear" is ready for a bear-b-q!

Artist: Matt Maletis, Racine

Matt Maletis has taught art at Giese Elementary School, Racine, for nine years. He coaches soccer at Washington Park High School and also coaches the U-11 Racine Soccer Club Red. He was the artist for *Cat Trick* in Cat'n Around Downtown. He thanks Phil Lyden, a retired teacher, who helped with *Bear-B-Q*. Lyden is active with Racine Theatre Guild.

Sponsor: Kewpee's Hamburgers

Bearstein

. . . celebrating Racine's food and beverage establishments.

Artist: John Ernst, West Allis, Wisconsin

John Ernst exhibits his work primarily in Southeastern Wisconsin galleries. His bold, abstract paintings incorporate vibrant colors that blend and balance the dimensions of depth, animation and texture, in an effort to establish an emotional connection with the viewer. He prefers a minimalist approach and strives to create works that evoke strong, positive feelings. He created *Polka Dot Cat* for Cat'n Around Downtown in 2003.

Sponsor: Evelyn's Club Main

Bee-hind Enemy Lines

. . . taking over the bees' hive and their honey.

Artist: Heather Brayer, Sturtevant, Wisconsin

Heather Brayer is a 1999 graduate of the University of Wisconsin-Parkside with a comprehensive art degree. She helps with art and photography for children's programs at Evangelical United Methodist Church. She also enjoys working on art projects at home with her husband and two young daughters. She and her husband participated in Cat'n Around Downtown.

Sponsor: Johnson Outdoors, Inc.

Bee-wary Bear

. . . going for the gold!

Artists: Jane Key and Mary Lou Dettmer, Racine
Jane Key is the owner of Racine's Inside/Out, a Chairities artist, an active member of Downtown Racine Corporation, and the silver winner of the Retailers Excellence Award for Visual Merchandising. Mary Lou Dettmer is a retired Western Publishing Company illustrator and editor. Her diverse career includes designing Hallmark cards and freelance work with Jim Henson and his Sesame Street characters. She participated in Cat'n Around Downtown.

Sponsor: Johnson Keland Management, Inc.

Gummy Bear

. . . overly fond of chewing gum.

Artist: Dina Gruber, Racine
Dina Gruber is the circulation sales manager for *The Journal Times* of Racine. Her favorite aspect of her position is working with teachers and students through the Newspapers in Education program and representing the newspaper at special events. She experimented with artwork as a hobby and has hand-painted glassware displayed and sold at Inside/Out of Racine.

Sponsor: Corner House

Nut 'n Honey

. . . sharing the treats.

Artist: Sheryl A. Meyer, Racine

Currently a pre-school teacher, Sheryl Meyer is a Racine native and William Horlick High School graduate. She studied interior design and enjoys a wide range of media. She has designed murals, logos and signage for local businesses. She has received honors in art contests in the United States and Japan. She participated in Dog Days of Summer and Cat'n Around Downtown, receiving high honors.

Sponsor: Martinizing Dry Cleaning

Paws for a Snack

. . . this North American black bear enjoys his snack.

Artist: Kathleen A. Lippold, Racine

A teacher in Racine Unified schools for more than 20 years, Kathleen Lippold works with special education students at the elementary level. She has always enjoyed art and considers it a challenge to create and work with many different kinds of media. She watercolor paints as a hobby. She participated in Cat'n Around Downtown.

Sponsor: Dick and Kathy Hansen

Picnic Partners

. . . intruding on a couple's picnic, and joined by a few friends.

Artist: Mary B. Sexton, Racine

Mary B. Sexton graduated from the Art Institute of Fort Lauderdale, Florida, with a bachelor of science degree in media arts and animation. In 2001, she moved to Racine after living in Florida for 28 years. She is a graphic designer who also utilizes different media such as animation, video production and editing for her creative outlets.

Sponsor: Red Onion Café

Strawbeari Shortcake

. . . part of a very special treat.

Artists: Claudia Rohling, Franksville, Wisconsin; Pam Lidington and Paul C. Rohling, Milwaukee

Claudia Rohling ran her own print and card company and has published two children's books. She is a clinical therapist at Lakeside Family Therapy and at Children's Service Society. Paul Rohling is a clinical therapist at The Therapy House and a graduate of Columbus (Ohio) College of Art and Design. Pam Lidington graduated from the University of Wisconsin-LaCrosse and is an executive director with the Laureate Group.

Sponsor: Culvers of Racine

Into the Berry Patch

*Bears and berries go well
together, given the bruins' love
of these fruits. These seven pay
tribute to a bear's favorite.*

Bear-ee-more

. . . like the bear's fur grows.

Artist: Lorna Hennig, Racine

Lorna Hennig holds a bachelor of fine arts degree from Cardinal Stritch University, Milwaukee, and also has done graduate work in art at the University of Wisconsin-Milwaukee. Her preferred media are watercolor, drawing and hand-made paper. Her work can be seen at the Artist Gallery and Mini Gallery in Racine, at Rivers Edge in Mishicot, Wisconsin, and the Anderson Arts Center in Kenosha.

Sponsor: Tri City National Bank

Berry Bear

. . . roaming through the berry patch nibbling on berries.

Artist: Kay Gregor, Racine

The executive director of the Racine Literacy Council since 1993, Kay Gregor has extensive background in the arts. She received her art degree from Mount Mary College in Milwaukee and a certificate in interior design from the Academy of Art, Chicago. She worked as an interior designer for several years and also taught art education at several local schools.

Sponsor: Thermal Transfer Products

Berry Go Round

. . . this panda loves his berries.

Artist: Kelly Drumm, Racine

Kelly Drumm, a Racine native and William Horlick High School 2002 graduate, attends the University of Wisconsin-Milwaukee, majoring in journalism and minoring in art. She spent four summers working as an artist within the Racine Parks, Recreational and Cultural Department's Main Gallery, where her pieces raised money at charity auctions held the end of each summer. She participated in Dog Days of Summer and Cat'n Around Downtown.

Sponsor: A-1 Auto Body

Jam"Beary"

. . . inspired by the children's book of the same-sounding name.

Artist: Jane Batten, Racine

A Racine native, Jane Batten graduated from St. Catherine's High School, then received her bachelor of science degree from the University of Wisconsin-LaCrosse, and her master's degree in education from National Louis University. Both a wife and mother, her interests include tennis, biking, art, animals, friends, family, community, travel and reading.

Sponsor: Twin Disc, Inc.

Raspbeary

. . . a huge berry, complete with foliage.

Artist: Megan Clausen, Racine

A 2004 graduate of Washington Park High School, Megan Clausen is now studying graphic design at Gateway Technical College. She enjoys many types of art. The biggest influences in her art and life have been her grandmother and fiance, Ted Matelski. She plans to keep art an active part of her future. She participated in Cat'n Around Downtown.

Sponsor: Nu-Wood Cabinet, Ltd.

Straw Beary

. . . ripe and emerging from the berry patch.

Artists: Linda Schubring, Sue Causey and Katy Diekfuss, Racine
Linda Schubring and Sue Causey, both full-time Realtors with Coldwell Banker and part-time arts aficionados, participated in the past two public-art projects – Dog Days of Summer and Cat'n Around Downtown – and are staunch supporters of the arts and the community. Katy Diekfuss, Schubring's daughter, is a native Racinian and a talented artist who also contributed her talents to the dog and cat projects.

Sponsor: Coldwell Banker Residential Brokerage

Strawbearry

. . . looks good enough to eat.

Artists: The Sklba Family, Racine
The entire Sklba family, all Racine natives, had their hands in this public-art project, including dad Christopher, mom Stephanie and children Jessica and Lauren. Chris, a graduate of Milwaukee Institute of Art and Design, is a professional goldsmith. He participated in Dog Days of Summer and Cat'n Around Downtown. Stephanie is employed at Gateway Technical College and Jessica and Lauren attend Jefferson Lighthouse Elementary School.

Sponsors: Charles and Joan Patton

Just For Fun

Traveling. Reading tarot cards.
Playing with marbles. Smiling – a lot.
These 12 bears are totally relishing the
fun they are having.

The Artful Traveler

. . . art, whimsy, color and loads of fun.

Artist: Paula D. Christensen, Cedarburg, Wisconsin
A 1985 graduate of the Milwaukee Institute of Art and Design, Paula Christensen is the visual art director of North Shore Academy of the Arts in Grafton, Wisconsin. She also operates a freelance studio, Paula's Palette. She has done graduate work at the School of the Museum of Fine Art in Boston, and exhibits her work throughout the Midwest.

Sponsor: Norman and Lynn Monson

Bear in Mind

. . . ce psychique ours recanter tout. (. . . these psychic bears tell all.)

Artist: Maggie Anne Berndt, Burlington, Wisconsin
Maggie Berndt is 16 years old and in her junior year at Burlington High School. She likes to paint, draw and be creative. She spends a lot of her time with horses and with little kids. She enjoys being outside, especially in the rain. She is learning how to read Tarot cards but admits to not being totally proficient at it.

Sponsor: Racine County Economic Development Corporation

Bizarro (the Bear)

. . . a clown inspired from the book Step Right This Way.

Artist: Jared Joslin on behalf of Cowpainters LLC, Chicago
Jared Joslin is a Chicago artist, represented by galleries in New York and Seattle. Joslin graduated from The Art Institute of Chicago in 1994. His work has been published in many fine arts periodicals and has received national awards. He participated in *Cows on Parade* and *Suite Home Chicago.*

Sponsor: Knight-Barry Title, Inc.

Blue Bear Mountain Marble Maze

. . . an interactive sculpture that invites participation.

Artist: Robert W. Andersen, Racine
A Racine native, Robert Andersen has been an art teacher in the Racine Unified School District since 1972 and an active local artist for three decades. A graduate of Washington Park High School, he received his bachelor of science degree in art from the University of Wisconsin-Whitewater and his masters degree in education from Carthage College, Kenosha. Andersen participated in Dog Days of Summer and Cat'n Around Downtown.

Sponsor: Sustainable Racine

Gazing Bear

. . . a garden gazing ball in the shape of a bear, with lights, flowers and dragonfly heads.

Artist: Tammy Easton, Racine

Tammy Easton has a degree in commercial art and is currently studying website design and animation at University of Wisconsin-Parkside. A freelance graphic designer, she has done decorative painting and participated in several craft shows exhibiting jewelry and clothing, "Tammy's Jewels". Her mosaic designs are shown at a local gallery and she has done many commissioned projects. She participated in Dog Days of Summer.

Sponsor: Jean and Phil Jacobson

Grin and Bear It

. . . a nervous circus bear doing his balancing act.

Artists: Karen, Krista and Becca Johnson, Racine

Karen Johnson is the owner of Aha! Studios, a Racine animation studio. Her daughters, Krista and Becca, share her love of art and animation. Krista, a recent graduate of the University of Wisconsin-Madison School of Journalism, is a marketing and event planner at Historic Century Market, Racine. Becca, a junior at William Horlick High School, is involved in student government and soccer and plans to study veterinary medicine.

Sponsor: Waters Edge Clothiers

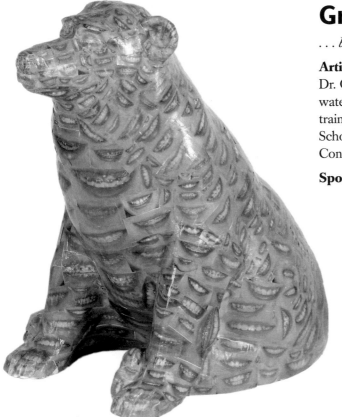

Grin and Bear It!

. . . beautiful smiles all over.

Artists: Gary W. Chu and Brianna Chu, Racine

Dr. Gary Chu took art courses in undergraduate school and enjoys watercolors. Daughter Brianna, in seventh grade, has been artistically trained through classes at Stephen Bull Fine Arts School and The Prairie School, both in Racine. Her work has been displayed at the Wingspread Conference Center and Charles A. Wustum Museum of Fine Arts.

Sponsor: Gary W. Chu, DDS, MS

Mardi Grrrras!

. . . Toby the polar bear enjoying the warmth and fun of New Orleans.

Artists: Megan Hunt, Racine, and Heather Johnson, Oak Creek, Wisconsin

Megan Hunt and Heather Johnson, both native Racinians, are collaborating artists and 1998 graduates of Washington Park High School. Hunt graduated in 2002 from The School of the Art Institute in Chicago with a fine arts degree. Johnson graduated from Milwaukee Institute of Art and Design in 2002 and is currently attending Mount Mary College, Milwaukee, earning her master's degree in art therapy.

Sponsor: N. Christensen & Son

Paint by Numbear

. . . a work in progress.

Artist: Jeani Berndt, Burlington, Wisconsin

Jeani Berndt is a freelance graphic designer and sometime art teacher. She has taught at Gateway Technical College and many area grade schools. She is currently working on a Website to showcase some of her odd creations. She, her husband and five children live on a farm in rural Burlington.

Sponsor: Econoprint of Racine

Panda Pagoda

. . . enjoying his elaborate domicile.

Artists: Kelly Gallaher and Children from Families with Children from China/Racine Chapter

Kelly Gallaher has been an active artist-in-residence in Racine area schools for almost a decade. Working in a variety of media – from ceramics to metal sculpture, murals and mosaics – Gallaher specializes in creating large-scale art events for school-age children. Gallaher and several children participated in Cat'n Around Downtown.

Sponsors: Dr. D. Kontra and Dr. D. Kruse

Rocking Bear

. . . a true bear back ride!

Artist: Amy Zahalka, Wind Lake, Wisconsin

Amy Zahalka received her art degree from the University of Wisconsin-Madison. She has worked in graphics and visual merchandising. Since returning to the Midwest, she earned her teaching certificate from the University of Wisconsin-Milwaukee and began teaching art in Racine. She participated in Dog Days of Summer and Cat'n Around Downtown.

Sponsor: Racine Heritage Museum

Santa Bear

. . . the perfect Santa Claus.

Artist: Amy J. Davis, Racine

Amy Davis and her family moved to Racine in 2002. Originally from Ohio, she has a degree in graphic design. Her preferred media are pencil, and pen and ink with watercolor wash. She is an instructor with the Young Rembrandts, a company designed to bring out the artist in children. She also loves to sing.

Sponsor: Nordik of America

67

Lively Arts

The arts play a significant role in our lives. So, too, with these 19 bears, who represent literature, the fine arts, sculpture, film, culture and more.

Bare Witness Holmes

. . . on the hunt for the culprit.

Artist: Lynn Spleas, Geneva Township, Wisconsin

Lynn Spleas has an associate degree in commercial art and accounting from Milwaukee Area Technical College. She currently works for the village of Waterford as a municipal deputy clerk/treasurer. She has had a lifelong passion for the arts. Her current ongoing project is redesigning and remodeling her home interior and exterior. She likes working with pen and ink and painting with acrylics.

Sponsor: St. Lucy Catholic Church

Bearded Bard of Beara

. . . a tribute to the Irish/Celtic culture.

Artist: Julie San Felipe, New Berlin, Wisconsin

A lifelong artist, Julie San Felipe teaches Celtic calligraphy at the Irish Cultural and Heritage Center in Milwaukee. She has developed a line of greeting cards and prints. Her art usually reflects the influence of her Irish heritage and her involvement in Irish cultural activities in Milwaukee. Her favorite media are calligraphy, words and poetry, and painting in watercolor and oil.

Sponsor: ZebraFeet Gallery

Bearnini Fountain

. . . patterned after a figure from Bernini's Fontana del Moro.

Artist: Darin Weisensel, Racine

A Racine native, Darin Weisensel is a freelance industrial designer and illustrator, holding a degree from the Milwaukee Institute of Art and Design. He enjoys illustrating children's books for Disney, DreamWorks, 20th Century Fox and Golden Books, in addition to projects for Warner Bros., Case, Trek and Miller. In his spare time he's the bassist for his church choir and the local band, Fur Pants.

Sponsor: Jazzercise on the Northside

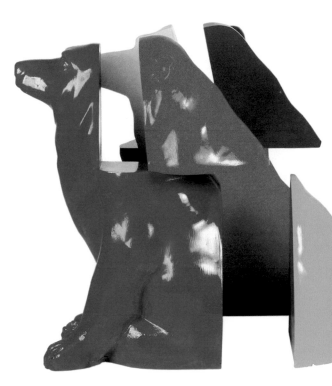

Bear Minimum

. . . inspired from minimalist painting and sculpture of the 1960s.

Artist: Christopher Dembroski, Chicago

A Racine native, Christopher Dembroski received his bachelor's degree in fine arts from the Milwaukee Institute of Art and Design. He is the co-owner of a Chicago-based design, building and renovation firm. His artwork is exhibited in numerous galleries throughout the Midwest and in permanent collections at Wingspread and the Johnson International Building in Racine.

Sponsor: E. C. Styberg Engineering Co., Inc.

Bear-ly Warhol

. . . the whimsy of Andy Warhol.

Artist: Timothy Carls, Racine

A Racine native and a University of Wisconsin-Parkside graduate, Timothy Carls is an artist and graphic designer employed by Design Partners, Inc. In his spare time he designs and produces vinyl cut graphics for signage. Currently he is creating a series of works using the vinyl, and has incorporated that style into his bear, as he did with his cat for Cat'n Around Downtown.

Sponsor: Design Partners, Inc.

24 GIANT SIZE PKGS.

24 GIANT SIZE PKGS.

New!

New!

Brillo®

Brillo®

Soap pads
WITH RUST RESISTER

Soap pads
WITH RUST RESISTER

BRILLO MFG. INC. MADE IN U.S.A.

SHINES ALUMINUM FAST

Blooh Bear

. . . inspired by the infamous Pooh, who was extraordinarily fond of honey.

Artist: Nancy Kellogg, Racine

Nancy Kellogg is a pre-med student preparing to enter Racine's Midwest College of Oriental Medicine. A fledgling "beek" with the Racine/Kenosha Beekeeper's Association, she is founding a co-op community-supported agriculture apiary to support local beekeepers. Kellogg's art training includes Milwaukee's Layton School of Art and Gateway Technical College's graphic design program. Blooh Bear uses the cyanotype (blueprint photographic) process and illustrates a passion for bees.

Sponsor: Brandt Jewelers

Beary Abstract

. . . abstract art with varied colors, shapes and patterns.

Artist: Kelly Witte, Racine

A 16-year-old high honors junior at William Horlick High School, Kelly Witte has been interested in art since she was a young child. During her freshman year, two of her works were exhibited in the Racine Unified School District exhibit at Charles A. Wustum Museum of Fine Arts, with one of the pieces also exhibited at Wingspread. She plans to pursue a degree in fine arts.

Sponsor: Johnson Financial Group

China Bear

. . . inspired from imagery found on Asian fabric and porcelain.

Artist: Sarah Mosk on behalf of Cowpainters LLC, Chicago

Sarah Mosk is the main designer for Cowpainters LLC of Chicago. She received her bachelor of fine art degree from Northern Illinois University. Upon graduating from school in 2000, Mosk dedicated her time to world travel. A recent trip to Asia directly influenced her design for *China Bear*. Painted in acrylic, the shapes and colors depict scenes often used in Eastern arts and crafts.

Sponsors: David and Terry Rayburn

Goldilocks and the 38 Kinder-Bears

. . . each student gets into the act.

Artists: Christine Pearson, Franksville, Wisconsin, and The Prairie School Kindergarteners, Racine

Christine Pearson has taught primary and middle school art at The Prairie School for 16 years. She has her bachelor of arts degree in art education from Augustana College in Rock Island, Illinois. She enjoys painting, drawing and gardening. Each of her 38 kindergarten students created a small bear to adorn this Goldilocks.

Sponsor: The Zaleski Family

73

Grin and Bear It

. . . famous smiles from a variety of great masters.

Artist: Tanya Fuhrman, Waterford, Wisconsin

Tanya Fuhrman studied art at the University of Wisconsin-Whitewater and University of Wisconsin-Milwaukee. A special education aide with autistic children in the Racine public schools, she has painted murals for churches, businesses and private homes. She also accepts commissions for stained glass artwork. She participated in Dog Days of Summer.

Sponsor: Montfort's Fine Art

Just Right

. . . has decided Goldilocks had more fun, so gives that role a try.

Artists: Heather Bumstead, Racine, and Laurie Gerber, Caledonia, Wisconsin

Heather Bumstead is director of pastoral care and a chaplain with Lincoln Lutheran of Racine. A self-taught artist, Bumstead admits to a passion for public art. Laurie Gerber is a registered nurse and director of nursing at Lincoln Village, Racine. A Caledonia native, she is an artist with needle and thread and has dressed everything imaginable. Bumstead participated in Dog Days of Summer and Cat'n Around Downtown.

Sponsor: Lincoln Lutheran of Racine

Lions and Tigers and Bears, Oh My!

. . . the big black bear poses no threat to the folks on their way to Oz.

Artist: Angela Perrault, Racine

Lifelong Racine resident Angela Perrault is a freelance artist and registered nurse. She expresses her creativity through watercolors, acrylics, calligraphy, rubber stamping, scrap booking, wall treatments and murals. Her preferred subjects include landscapes, portraits and florals. She works part-time on the surgical and orthopedic units at Saint Mary's Medical Center. Her feline creation for Cat'n Around Downtown, *CATerpillar,* earned an honorable mention.

Sponsor: Nielsen Machine Co., Inc.

Lions and Tigers ON Bears, Oh My!

. . . a pun on the line from "Wizard of Oz."

Artist: Heather Bumstead, Racine

Heather Bumstead is the director of pastoral care and a chaplain with Lincoln Lutheran of Racine. A self-taught artist, Bumstead admits to a particular passion for public art because it is interactive and "shows people that art isn't just the 'Mona Lisa.' It comes in many forms and fashions. It's all around us." Bumstead participated in Dog Days of Summer and Cat'n Around Downtown.

Sponsor: All Saints Healthcare

Little Bear Blue

. . . creating an atmosphere of cool yet soft and approachable distance.

Artist: Marti Anderson, Milwaukee

An early childhood special needs teacher for the Milwaukee Public Schools, Marti Anderson enjoys creating liturgical art, singing, acting, gardening, reading, writing, socializing, laughing and learning. Life and art are exciting adventures for her and she often experiments with new art forms and materials, whether working on canvas, paper, fabric or furniture. Her art has been displayed in juried shows at university campuses and at the Janesville, Wisconsin, Rotary Gardens.

Sponsor: Erickson Auto Trim

Little Bear, the Storyteller

. . . the Wadewitz grizzly is the storyteller of the legend of Polaris, the north star.

Artist: Catherine A. Gister, M.ed., Racine

Catherine Gister, art specialist at Wadewitz Elementary School for 30 years, dedicates *Little Bear*, the Wadewitz mascot, to her past, present and future students. The bear encourages students to look to Polaris, the star symbolizing William Horlick High School. Scholarship, service, leadership, integrity and teamwork represent the star's points. In her studio overlooking her garden and the Root River, Gister pursues her interests in folk art, ceramics and children's book illustration.

Sponsor: Advanced Garage Door Service

Russian Bear

. . . the bear, one of the symbols of Russia, with little bears reminiscent of the Metrolska doll.

Artist: Tanya Fuhrman, Waterford, Wisconsin

Tanya Fuhrman studied art at the University of Wisconsin-Whitewater and University of Wisconsin-Milwaukee. A special education aide with autistic children in the Racine public schools, she has painted murals for churches, businesses and private homes. She also accepts commissions for stained glass artwork. She participated in Dog Days of Summer.

Sponsor: Clifton Gunderson LLP

Serenity

. . . depicting calm for contemplation of the arts.

Artist: Catherine Wellman, Oshkosh, Wisconsin

Catherine Wellman holds fine art degrees in photography, drawing and art education. She has been an artist for 15 years and is currently teaching in public schools in the Oshkosh area. Wellman has presented many local and national workshops on Polaroid photography and is pursuing a masters in bookmaking. She works in metal and wood also.

Sponsor: Spa at Great Lakes

Sir Bearlock Holmes

. . . the solution to the mystery is near.

Artist: Amy J. Davis, Racine

Amy Davis and her family moved to Racine in 2002. Originally from Ohio, she has a degree in graphic design. Her preferred media are pencil, and pen and ink with watercolor wash. She is an instructor with the Young Rembrandts, an organization designed to bring out the artist in children. She also loves to sing.

Sponsor: Young Rembrandts - A Children's Drawing Program

Tigger Pooh

. . . Pooh dresses the part of Tigger's lost brother.

Artist: Anthony B. Sanchez, Racine

A Racine native and Washington Park High School graduate, Anthony Sanchez never left the city of his birth. Stencil drawings of ancient ruins and castles are a passion of this realist painter. Tigger Pooh is the first public art project the artist has undertaken.

Sponsor: Bank One

Magical Music

*Music brings joy into the
lives of these seven musically
inclined bruins.*

The Bear with Kaleidoscope Eyes

. . . a Beatle-esque theme inspired by her infant son's love of the Beatles.

Artist: Mishell Sommer-Bayer, Milwaukee

A proud mom, wife and artist, Mishell Sommer-Bayer was an art specialist for the Boys and Girls Clubs of Milwaukee for six years. She has been commissioned for painting and sculpture by private and public funders. She earned her bachelor of arts degree in art therapy from Mount Mary College, Milwaukee. She enjoys making art, practicing tai chi and being with family and friends.

Sponsor: Mainstream Music

Bear-a-Tone

. . . plenty of sheet music from which to choose.

Artist: Mary Elizabeth Nelson, Racine

Mary Nelson is an oncology certified registered nurse at All Saints Cancer Center who has a creative passion. She has done many personal commissions for family and friends. Her preferred media are decoupage, photography and floral design. She finds the color, texture and script found in antique sheet music intriguing and each piece on her bear is hand-torn and placed.

Sponsor: JobsinRacine.com

Bearatone

. . . the bear as both musical instrument and performer.

Artist: Barbara Lindquist, Racine
Barbara Lindquist, 73, has been making art for nearly 60 years. At 14, she was chosen to attend the Chicago Art Institute. At 18, she apprenticed to a violin maker and she has been making musical instruments since then. She works in all media and her creations are in private collections worldwide. A partner in Mother Courage Press, she helped produce 25 books. She participated in Cat'n Around Downtown.

Sponsor: Sierra Inc.

Blue Bear's Band

... "Section 8" is here, on one body.

Artist: Joan Houlehen, Cudahy, Wisconsin
A graphic artist/designer, Joan Houlehen is a partner in A. Houberbocken, Inc., an art consulting firm. An abstractionist working in oil and tempera, she is a docent at Haggerty Museum of Art on the Marquette University campus and on the board of directors of Friends of the Haggerty. She has judged many shows in the Midwest, and participated in Dog Days of Summer and Cat'n Around Downtown.

Sponsor: George's Tavern

Fat Dominoes on Mr. Blue Beary Hill

... whimsical variation of a '50s hit.

Artist: Violet O'Dell, Racine
Violet O'Dell, the artist of BrokenWingStudio, works in various media. Though mostly self-taught, she took courses at Charles A. Wustum Museum of Fine Arts during her high school years. She currently is working on a series for breast cancer victims and survivors and submitted her ideas for the World Trade Center memorial. She participated in Dog Days of Summer and Cat'n Around Downtown.

Sponsor: Sharon Hill, DC

Grateful the Dancing Bear

. . . mascot for the famed Dead Heads.

Artist: Danelle D. Schultz, Racine
Danelle Schultz is the owner/director of Dance Arts Center, Franksville, Wisconsin, where she teaches ballet, jazz and tap to more than 300 children. She holds the title of Mrs. Wisconsin 2002 and enjoyed making the majority of her title appearances in the Downtown Racine area. Her other artistic interests include painting and decorating. She participated in Cat'n Around Downtown.

Sponsor: Dance Arts Center/The Hair Connection

Jimmy Bearffet from Marbearitaville

. . . but can this bear sing?

Artists: Pat Malmstadt and Carmen Warren, Racine
Collaborators Pat Malmstadt and Carmen Warren are a crafty duo with a fetish for details. They both enjoy challenging projects, including painting, stitching, sewing and jewelry. Afflicted with an affection for bears of all kinds, Malmstadt is office manager for Accutemp Mechanical and is known for cleverness, creativity and wide imagination. A mom of two sons with a degree in elementary education, Warren is known for her original designs.

Sponsor: Warren Eye Care Center

Native American Tributes

The bear was a significant force
in Native American culture.
This importance is portrayed with
these four bears.

Bearing My Soul

. . . the significance of the bear and the seven elements in Native American culture.

Artist: Candace Walters, Buffalo Grove, Illinois

Candace Walters is a professional graphic designer and graduate of the Rhode Island School of Design. She has a passion for sculpture created in all forms of media and enjoys making her own when she is able. *Kittyhawk*, her contribution to Cat'n Around Downtown, earned high honors recognition.

Sponsor: Design Partners, Inc.

Indian Spirits

. . . the bear as the powerful symbol of Native American life.

Artist: Rosemary Curtin, Racine

Born and raised near North Carolina's Outer Banks, Rosemary Curtin feels at home with Lake Michigan in her backyard. Her studies include courses at Milwaukee Institute of Art and Design and workshops with artists here and in Pennsylvania. Her studio is above Spectrum Art Gallery. She and her husband are restoring a 155-year-old Greek Revival house in Racine's historic district. She participated in Cat'n Around Downtown.

Sponsor: Quick Cable Corporation

Northwest Coast Bear

. . . black bear inspired by the art of Northwest Coast Indians.

Artist: Kristin Gjerdset, Milwaukee

An associate professor of art at Wisconsin Lutheran College, Milwaukee, Kristin Gjerdset finds it essential to travel to natural places to facilitate growth in her artwork, to stay inspired and to make others aware of the need for environmental preservation. In 2004, she was selected as an artist-in-residence at Everglades National Park in Florida. She participated in Cat'n Around Downtown.

Sponsor: Avenue Gallery and Frame

Spirit Bear

. . . a tribute to the Native American custom of adorning likenesses of animal figures as fetishes.

Artist: Marj Lacock, Racine

Marj Lacock received her fine arts degree from the University of Wisconsin-Parkside. She currently works with watercolors on paper or canvas; enhancing the images with colored pencils, metallic leaf and beads. Her works have appeared in Southeastern Wisconsin invitational and juried exhibitions. She is a member of Artists Gallery, Racine, and exhibits at Funky Hannah's, Racine, and Seebeck Gallery, Kenosha. She participated in Cat'n Around Downtown.

Sponsor: Wisconsin Health and Fitness/World Gym

Spectacular Sports

*Fishing, biking, sledding, surfing,
golfing, even baseball and football.
These 13 bears enjoy it all.*

The Big Bearhuna

. . . go out and enjoy the lake and work on keeping it clean for all to enjoy!

Artists: Tom Ward and Matt Andis, Racine, and Todd Fillingham, Milwaukee

All three artists are avid lake surfers. A Racine native, Matt Andis is a Carthage College graduate. He is a former Western Lake Michigan director of the Surf Rider Foundation. New Jersey native Tom Ward, animation director at Aha! Studios, has lived in Racine since 1986. He is a member of Racine's Keep Our Beaches Open. Todd Fillingham is a custom furniture maker and artist, and a sailor as well as surfer.

Sponsor: Andis Company

Bear With It

. . . enjoying a comical winter sledding moment.

Artist: Shawna Williams, Racine

Racine native Shawna Williams is 21 years old and graduated in 2000 from Gateway Technical College. She is employed in customer service/sales at *The Journal Times*. She loves animals and spends time volunteering and rescuing animals within the Racine area. She has been creative all her life and has been playing the violin for 13 years.

Sponsor: Express Personnel

Biker-Bear

. . . all set to hit the road.

Artist: Daniel McConnell, Racine

Daniel McConnell is a retired graphic artist. He received his bachelor of arts degree from Layton School of Art, Milwaukee, and during his career held several graphics positions, including those with the U.S. Army and the Wisconsin Department of Education. He enjoys building and collecting model cars, model railroading, photography and travel. He plans to launch a new book this year.

Sponsor: Rochelle and Robb Ehrhart

Cubby Bear

. . . paying homage to the Chicago Cubs.

Artist: Julie Lynam, Racine

Julie Lynam, a native of Racine, attended the University of Wisconsin-Stout and earned a degree in art education. She now teaches art at Wind Point and Winslow elementary schools in Racine. Her favorite medium is painting on canvas. She also enjoys rubber stamping and scrapbooking. She participated in Dog Days of Summer and Cat'n Around Downtown.

Sponsor: Goebel Electric, Inc.

Fat Boy

. . . for the love of biking.

Artist: Frank Cihler, Racine

Racine native Frank Cihler is the father of three daughters, the youngest now serving in the armed forces. His works have been shown in galleries in New York and Las Vegas and in Racine's Charles A. Wustum Museum of Fine Arts. His cigar art was featured in a recent article in *Twenty One* magazine. Other works include celebrity portraits, pirates, ships and his *Blue Lady* paintings.

Sponsor: Metro Milwaukee Auto Auction

Fish'n Bear

. . . all set for a day on the water.

Artist: Rachel A. Womack, Slinger, Wisconsin

Born and raised in Racine, Rachel Womack graduated from William Horlick High School. She received her bachelor of science degree from Carroll College, Waukesha, with a major in journalism and a minor in art. Her free time is spent hand-carving fish and painting wildlife for Timber Lodge Gallery in Hartford, Wisconsin. She and her husband Todd enjoy hiking and fishing the local and area lakes.

Sponsor: Ivanhoe Pub and Eatery

Golden Bear

. . . a tribute to golfing great Jack Nicklaus.

Artist: Bonita Carbajal, Racine

A native of Stevens Point, Wisconsin, Bonita Carbajal studied architecture and art history at the University of Wisconsin-Milwaukee. She works in oil, charcoal and watercolor, and does papier mache sculpture using recycled materials. She participated in Dog Days of Summer and Cat'n Around Downtown.

Sponsor: Bob Randleman

Gone Fishing

. . . he knows how to get those rainbow trout.

Artist: Renee Popadic, Racine

Born and raised in Racine, Renee Popadic has always enjoyed all types of arts and crafts. She especially enjoys drawing, sculpting and painting wildlife. Popadic's favorite hobby is woodcarving. She is president of Racine's Wildlife Carving Club. She participated in Dog Days of Summer and Cat'n Around Downtown.

Sponsor: Metro Racine Safety Enforcement, LLC

If You Can't Beat 'em, Join 'em

. . . this bear has changed his allegiance and roots for the Packers instead.

Artist: Paul Muckler, Oak Creek, Wisconsin

Paul Muckler has always enjoyed being creative. He draws and paints, and works in a variety of media. Music, sports and reading comprise some of his other interests. Previous exhibitions include Milwaukee's Beastie Beat and Pigs in the Park, and Racine's Cat'n Around Downtown. He also created artwork for the Channel 10 PBS auction. Muckler is a graduate of the University of Wisconsin-Milwaukee.

Sponsor: The Bellwether Corporation

Sunny Sam

. . . sunny skies, bright and cheery, perfect day for fishing.

Artist: Teri Vandenhoven, Milwaukee

A native of Green Bay, Wisconsin, Teri Vandenhoven is an emerging artist with formal education from the University of Wisconsin-Green Bay. She has been in three juried shows at the University of Wisconsin-Milwaukee and has had her abstract paintings on display at other galleries. She is a bear lover and is from a family of fishermen. She enjoys other outdoor activities and is a veteran marathon runner.

Sponsor: CRB Insurance

Surfer Dude

. . . this polar bear chillin' in the warm sun and surf.

Artist: Evette Sapp-Nasr, Chaska, Minnesota

Evette Sapp-Nasr is a University of Wisconsin-Parkside fine arts graduate. She has participated in various shows and competitions. A Kenosha native now living in Minnesota, she enjoys painting and drawing in her free time. She participated in Cat'n Around Downtown.

Sponsor: Great Lakes Yacht Services Corp.

"Sweetness"

. . . in memory of Chicago Bears great Walter Payton.

Artist: Russell E. Asala, Racine

Russell Asala, a graduate of Northwestern University, began his career at SC Johnson and subsequently owned two art and design studios: Creative Concepts, Inc., and Phoenix Design Group, Inc. While now retired, Asala does substitute teaching at the elementary school level. Among his hobbies are art, cooking and gardening. He participated in Cat'n Around Downtown.

Sponsor: Nicholas Industries

Wrigley Rocks Racine

. . . "Put me in, Coach. I'm ready to play in Downtown Racine!"

Artist: Karen A. Johnston, Racine

Janesville, Wisconsin, native Karen Johnston received her bachelor's degree in art education from the University of Wisconsin-Madison and a master of fine arts from Southern Illinois University, where she also taught. Formerly a K-12 art teacher and University of Wisconsin-Parkside adjunct professor, she continues her work in ceramic sculpture and operates One O.A.K. Design, a multi-media enterprise, from her home studio. Her ceramic sculpture has been exhibited in several Midwestern shows.

Sponsor: Project Management Associates

The Ultimate Universe

The infinite universe gives us beauty, mystery, the necessities and wonders of life, as shown with these 14 bears.

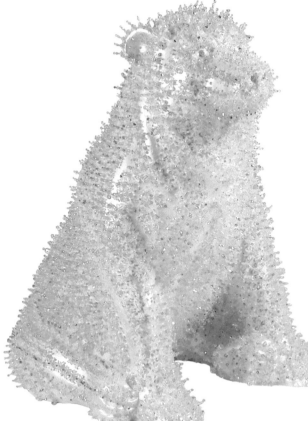

Aurora Bearealis

. . . tiny crystals and twinkling lights portray the northern lights.

Artist: Rebecca Bissi-Bloom, Racine

Rebecca Bissi-Bloom holds a bachelor of science degree in textiles from the University of Georgia and a bachelor of fine arts in fashion design from the Art Institute of Chicago. She worked for 10 years as a fashion designer in Chicago and Hong Kong. She moved to Racine in 1988 with her family and enjoys donating her talents to The Prairie School Premiere. She participated in Cat'n Around Downtown with *Palm Beach Cat.*

Sponsor: Mathis Gallery Frame Shop

Aurora Bearealis

. . . the sweep of color, northern sky beauty.

Artists: Erin Hopkins, Racine, and Susan Goergen, Kenosha, Wisconsin

Erin Hopkins and Susan Goergen are art students at the University of Wisconsin-Parkside. Goergen, 20, admits to an abnormally large shoe collection. Hopkins, 24 is an animal person; not an item in her closet is without dog, cat or horse hair. They both love painting, the Harry Potter books and visiting art museums.

Sponsor: A & E Incorporated

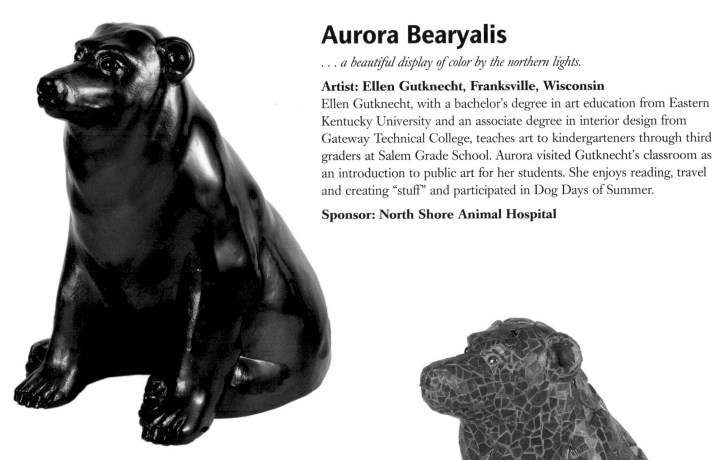

Aurora Bearyalis

. . . a beautiful display of color by the northern lights.

Artist: Ellen Gutknecht, Franksville, Wisconsin

Ellen Gutknecht, with a bachelor's degree in art education from Eastern Kentucky University and an associate degree in interior design from Gateway Technical College, teaches art to kindergarteners through third graders at Salem Grade School. Aurora visited Gutknecht's classroom as an introduction to public art for her students. She enjoys reading, travel and creating "stuff" and participated in Dog Days of Summer.

Sponsor: North Shore Animal Hospital

The Bare Necessities

. . . each star represents life's necessities: air, water, food, time, rest, play and love.

Artist: Denise Roberts McKee, Racine

Denise Roberts McKee is chief operating officer and partner of Stunt Puppy Entertainment, Inc., a developer of children's software. She also co-owns Working Dog Gallery LLC, a gallery of contemporary artworks located in Racine's Historic Sixth Street Arts District. Her mixed media mosaic work has won awards, the most recent being first place in Racine's Cat'n Around Downtown competition.

Sponsor: Working Dog Gallery LLC

Bears of the World

. . . bears know no lines or human laws for their protection.

Artists: Tonya Lambeth Dilley and David Dilley, Racine

This husband-wife team created *Bears of the World*. Tonya Lambeth Dilley holds a bachelor of fine arts degree from the University of Wisconsin-Parkside. Her works range from oil paintings to fiber projects. David Dilley is a professionally trained carpenter. He is a woodworker with a specialty in custom musky lures. He enjoys musky fishing and deer hunting. She participated in Dog Days of Summer and both participated in Cat'n Around Downtown.

Sponsor: CNH

Buddha Bear

. . . depicts the essential elements found in the image of Buddha.

Artist: Reid A. Pfarr, Racine

Reid Pfarr holds a bachelor of arts degree in fine arts from the University of Wisconsin-Parkside. He works on a wide variety of art continuums, ranging from woodcarving, sculpture and drawing to restoring classic cars. Pfarr has won numerous awards for his auto restorations and wood carvings. He participated in Cat'n Around Downtown.

Sponsor: Associated Bank

Charla, Rainbow Glass Bear

. . . this polar bear reflects glassy light in her rainbow colors.

Artist: Betty H. Marquand, Racine

Colorado native Betty Marquand has lived in Racine since 1988.
Now retired, she had been a chaplain with All Saints Healthcare System.
She took classes at the University of Wisconsin-Parkside, specializing
in printmaking and ceramics. Her works are on permanent display at the
DeKoven Center. She has exhibited in juried shows and has had her
own shows at Spectrum Art Gallery and Racine Visitors
and Convention Bureau.

Sponsor: St. Luke's Episcopal Church

Globe Trotter

. . . showcases a globe, showing its diverse travels.

Artist: Peg Ducommun, Racine

Growing up in Antioch, Illinois, Peg Ducommun showed artistic talent
at a young age; at 14 began winning art contests and at 16 enjoyed
freelancing for private homes. She has won awards in shows throughout
Wisconsin and Illinois. She loves all forms of art and continues to pursue
her passion for the field. She participated in Dog Days of Summer and
Cat'n Around Downtown.

Sponsor: Myrna R. Bellomy

Ice Cubed

. . . braving the Arctic by making his own igloo.

Artist: Brooke Wentland, Madison, Wisconsin
Brooke Wentland graduated from the University of Wisconsin-Madison with a bachelor's degree in fine arts and graphic design concentration. This Green Bay area native is a graphic designer at Pacific Cycle, Inc. in Madison. Artistic interests include freelance design, watercolor, photography and decorative furniture painting. She participated in Cat'n Around Downtown.

Sponsor: Chuck and Jen Johnson

Snowflake

. . . no two snowflakes are the same.

Artist: Carla Marie Reed, Fall River, Wisconsin
Carla Reed holds a bachelor of science degree in nursing from Marian College in Fond du Lac, Wisconsin. She enjoys quilting, cross-stitch, drawing and painting. She has attempted a woodcarving with a chainsaw. She participated in Cat'n Around Downtown.

Sponsor: Bank of Elmwood

Sunny the Solar Polar

. . . brings warmth and light, gifted with radiant beauty.

Artist: Kate Remington, Racine

The proprietor of Remington-May workshop gallery in Downtown Racine, Kate Remington has been a practicing artist her entire adult life. Currently she spends most of her time creating custom concrete art sculpture and functional pieces. A graduate of Northwestern University, she was the founder of two Chicago cooperatives. She participated in Dog Days of Summer.

Sponsors: Donna and Marty Defatte and Sadiqua Hamdan

Ursa Major

. . . looking over and protecting Earth.

Artists: Leah Andersen and Nicole Yoghourtjian, Racine

This collaborative team consists of two aspiring artists. Leah Andersen is a junior at Washington Park High School. Nicole Yoghourtjian is a junior at Christian Life High School. Andersen, who grew up with art, plays soccer and tennis and is presently taking a sculpture class. Yoghourtjian has a scrapbook business, plays softball and is involved with art at school.

Sponsor: Putzmeister, Inc.

Ursa Major – The Great Bear

. . . the constellations sparkle in daylight and nighttime.

Artist: Jean Thielen, Racine

Jean Thielen is well-known for her paintings of the Wind Point lighthouse and scenes of Racine and Wisconsin. She currently teaches watercolor classes at the University of Wisconsin-Parkside. She has exhibited her paintings at many Wisconsin and Midwest shows and galleries, and has won numerous awards for her work, which appears in many corporate and private collections.

Sponsor: Racine County Convention and Visitors Bureau

Ursus Horribilis Aurora Borealis

. . . transformed into a dark night sky with the northern lights effect.

Artist: Robert W. Andersen, Racine

A Racine native, Robert Andersen has been an art teacher in the Racine Unified School District since 1972 and an active local artist for three decades. A graduate of Washington Park High School, he received his bachelor of science degree in art from the University of Wisconsin-Whitewater and his masters degree in education from Carthage College, Kenosha. Andersen participated in Dog Days of Summer and Cat'n Around Downtown.

Sponsor: Jim and Roberta Fiene

Wilderness Wanderings

Fourteen bears are found happily wandering through their varied wilderness habitats – needing to be preserved for the future – while also enjoying other outdoor places.

Aaaw, Mom, Just Five Weeks More!

. . . this bear cub resisting coming out of hibernation.

Artist: Violet O'Dell, Racine
Violet O'Dell, the artist of BrokenWingStudio, works in various media. Though mostly self-taught, she took courses at Charles A. Wustum Museum of Fine Arts during her high school years. She currently is working on a series for breast cancer victims and survivors and submitted her ideas for the World Trade Center memorial. She participated in Dog Days of Summer and Cat'n Around Downtown.

Sponsor: Educators Credit Union

Bear Hunt

. . . hidden behind branches with berries and birds.

Artist: Marian J. Kane, Prairie du Sac, Wisconsin
Marian Kane, a professional artist and primarily a painter, is a graduate of the School of Art Institute of Chicago, her native city. Her work is typically representational and involved with themes of perception, expectation and emotion. Her work has been shown at the Art Institute of Chicago, the Madison Art Center and the Milwaukee Art Museum. She participated in Dog Days of Summer.

Sponsor: Milaeger's

Bear-ly There

. . . the bear's environment displayed; we must not disturb his natural habitat and climate conditions.

Artist: Mickie Krueger, Racine

Mickie Krueger currently is program chair for the Racine Art Guild and is active in the local arts community. Her work has been shown at Charles A. Wustum Museum of Fine Arts in Racine and Anderson Art Gallery in Kenosha. She works in a variety of media, including oil, pastel and clay. Krueger's job experiences include silkscreen instructor and graphic artist. She participated in Cat'n Around Downtown.

Sponsor: Michael Westman, DDS, MS

Beral

. . . enjoying the surrounding vegetation.

Artist: Rachel Ballantyne, Racine

Rachel Ballantyne started sewing and crafting before the age of 5. She is very active with three-dimensional projects such as stage and costume design and implementation. Although mainly self-taught, she has taken classes at the University of Wisconsin-Parkside and Charles A. Wustum Museum of Fine Arts. She dedicates her bear in honor of her grandmother, Beral Hennings, whose artistic talents have always been a source of inspiration.

Sponsors: Elena and Nicholas Ruffo

"Bud"dy Bear

. . . buds and flowers are a reminder of a summertime garden.

Artist: Jodi Klug, Franksville, Wisconsin

Working part-time at SC Johnson and having a large family can be stressful! Painting is Jodi Klug's way of keeping everything in perspective. She has been decorative painting for more than 25 years and holds a holiday open house in her home. During the summer, she keeps busy in the garden and helps to run the Yorkville 4H food stand at the Racine County Fair.

Sponsor: Dr. Richard M. Wagner, Oral and Maxillo/Facial Surgery

The Call of the Wild

. . . captures the Rocky Mountain wildlife habitat.

Artist: Sue Horton, Franksville, Wisconsin

A Chicago native, Sue Horton earned a bachelor of science degree from Loyola University of Chicago. She is a registered nurse and artist. She enjoys working in acrylics, pastels and watercolors. Recent projects include murals and pastel landscapes, and painting bisque ware. She participated in Dog Days of Summer and Cat'n Around Downtown.

Sponsor: The Horton Family

Cubweb

. . . the beautiful web and its spiders shine on the cub's background.

Artist: Krista Lea Meinert Edquist, Fort Atkinson, Wisconsin

Shortly after Krista Lea Meinert Edquist received her fine arts degree from the University of Wisconsin-Parkside in 1998, she was commissioned to do multiple projects. In 2002 her photographs and sculptures were accepted for Charles A. Wustum Museum of Fine Arts' Tri-County Photographic Print Competition and Racine Area Arts Exhibition. She participated in Dog Days of Summer and Cat'n Around Downtown.

Sponsor: Dr. Clare B. Johnson

The Great Bearier Reef

. . . enjoying the magic of the ocean.

Artist: Tom Ward, Racine

Tom Ward is the animation director at Aha! Studios in Racine. He attended Parsons School of Design in New York City and is a 1985 graduate of Sheridan College's Character Animation program in Oakville, Ontario. A Racine resident since 1986, he enjoys sharing his knowledge with young artists. He has taught at Charles A. Wustum Museum of Fine Arts and has been the artist-in-residence at several schools.

Sponsor: Sign Pro-A Division of Pristine Products

The Great Bear-ier Reef

. . . the Big Kahuna will explore ocean coral and much, much more.

Artists: Russell E. Asala, Racine, and Marsha Sokel, Schaumburg, Illinois

Russell Asala is a retired art and design studio owner who currently substitute teaches in the Racine Unified school system. His hobbies include art, cooking and gardening. His sister Marsha Sokel is an accomplished and award-winning floral designer and craftsperson. Together they collaborated on and created *The Great Bear-ier Reef.*

Sponsor: Photographic Design, Ltd.

The Great Bearracuda

. . . rarely attacks a person wearing clothing.

Artist: Krista Lea Meinert Edquist, Fort Atkinson, Wisconsin

Shortly after Krista Lea Meinert Edquist received her fine arts degree from the University of Wisconsin-Parkside in 1998, she was commissioned to do multiple projects. In 2002 her photographs and sculptures were accepted for Charles A. Wustum Museum of Fine Arts' Tri-County Photographic Print Competition and Racine Area Arts Exhibition. She participated in Dog Days of Summer and Cat'n Around Downtown.

Sponsor: Diamond/Laser Services

The Great Northwoods

. . . all found in Wisconsin's northwoods.

Artist: Renee Popadic, Racine

Born and raised in Racine, Renee Popadic has always
enjoyed all types of arts and crafts. She especially enjoys
drawing, sculpting and painting wildlife. Popadic's favorite
hobby is woodcarving. She is president of Racine's Wildlife
Carving Club. She participated in Dog Days of Summer and
Cat'n Around Downtown.

Sponsors: Louie Seabolt and Jane Hutterly

Lilies and Tulips and Bears! Oh My!

. . . covered in flora typical of a Wisconsin garden.

Artists: Dorothy Smalancke, Racine and Amy Kratochvil, Wind Lake, Wisconsin

Dorothy Smalancke has been painting for more than 25 years and belongs to the National Society of Decorative Painters and a local painting chapter, Turp 'n' Stein. Granddaughter Amy Kratochvil, a Racine native, attended Horlick High School and earned her art education degree from the University of Wisconsin-Madison. She teaches elementary school art in Big Bend, Wisconsin. Smalancke participated in Dog Days of Summer.

Sponsors: John and Dianne Palmgren

Salmon Run

. . . brilliant red, easy and tasty prey for bears.

Artist: Kristin Gjerdset, Milwaukee

An associate professor of art at Wisconsin Lutheran College, Milwaukee, Kristin Gjerdset finds it essential to travel to natural places to facilitate growth in her artwork, to stay inspired and to make others aware of the need for environmental preservation. In 2004, she was selected as an artist-in-residence at Everglades National Park in Florida. She participated in Cat'n Around Downtown.

Sponsor: Merchants Moving and Storage Co.

What Does a Bear Do in the Woods?

. . . reading the morning paper.

Artist: Lauren DeMorrow, Racine

Lauren DeMorrow enjoys watercolor and oil painting, and welcomes opportunities to put her creativity to the test. She has an engineering degree and a master's degree in business administration. She currently works as a human resources manager, is the mother of one and an animal lover. She enjoys traveling and experiencing new things when time permits. She is excited about participating in this year's public art event.

Sponsor: Dover Flag and Map, LLC

The Working World

The world of work can present
challenges – and fulfillment –
as shown through these nine bears.

Bear Market

. . . lamenting the bear market in the early years of the 21st century.

Artists: Karen Johnson and Jill Sturino, Racine

Sisters Karen Johnson and Jill Sturino are Racine natives. Johnson is the owner of Aha! Studios (formerly Karen Johnson Productions) and is a co-owner of Stunt Puppy Entertainment. She has produced numerous children's computer games for Disney, Mattel, Hasbro Interactive and Fisher Price. Sturino is an executive assistant at SC Johnson and this is her second artistic endeavor. She also loves traveling and gardening.

Sponsor: Norco Manufacturing Corp.

Bearie Prairie

. . . emulating the architectural genius of Frank Lloyd Wright.

Artist: Lynn Jones, Racine

Lynn Jones has been immersed in art her entire life. Her father, an architect, was head of planning and construction at the University of Wisconsin-Parkside. With encouragement from her parents and nurturing teachers, she delved into many art forms and continued her studies at UW-Parkside. Her projects have been displayed at Charles A. Wustum Museum of Fine Arts. Recent accomplishments include card making, sewing and new beading techniques.

Sponsors: Jay and Ric Ruffo

Bear-er of Good News

. . . a smartly dressed newsboy.

Artist: Nathan R. Leininger, Oak Creek, Wisconsin
Racine native Nathan Leininger demonstrated artistic ability
from childhood. His work was chosen for Charles A. Wustum
Museum of Fine Arts exhibits. While serving in the U.S. Navy
as a medic, he used his talents for several projects, including a
representation of Aden, Yemen, for which he received a
commendation from the Fifth Fleet commander. He is now
studying at the University of Wisconsin-Milwaukee and
working at *The Business Journal*.

Sponsor: *The Business Journal*

Bearly Makin' It

. . . getting by as best he can.

Artists: Sarah Rabinowe and Alexandra Nilles, Racine
Sarah Rabinowe enjoys all aspects of art, from acrylic landscapes to
Victorian-era design. She is an eighth grade student at The Prairie
School, where she enjoys glass-blowing, ceramics and design. Alexandra
Nilles is a junior at St. Catherine's High School. She also attended The
Prairie School, where she enjoyed glass-blowing. She loves visiting
museums and participating in fine art projects.

Sponsor: WISPARK LLC

Buddy

. . . this superhero protects everyone.

Artist: Samantha Flock, Milwaukee

Samantha Flock is a junior at the University of Wisconsin-Milwaukee, majoring in art and minoring in biology. She plans to attend graduate school for medical illustration. Her favorite art is drawing super heroes, hence her idea for *Buddy*. She has painted murals and during second semester 2004, her works were in two exhibits: Heroines and Hellions at the UWM Union and the Foundations Show at UWM.

Sponsor: Racine Family YMCA

Farmer Bear

. . . enjoying his work in the out-of-doors.

Artist: Dorothy Popadic, Racine

Dorothy Popadic is a lifelong resident of Racine. She enjoys doing a variety of arts and crafts, among them knitting, crocheting and ceramics. She has donated crocheted lap robes to Racine area nursing homes, and knitted hats and mittens for children to various charities. She and her daughter Renee participated in the 2002 Festival of Trees when they handcrafted whimsical snowmen ornaments.

Sponsor: Historic Century Market

LumBearjack

. . . all about working in the woods.

Artists: Kim Nelson and Daun Johnson, Franksville, Wisconsin, and Union Grove (Wisconsin) High School Students

This burly bear is the creation of Union Grove High School students, led by Kim Nelson and Daun Johnson. Their prior artistic endeavors include designing and decorating trees for Racine's Festival of Trees in 2002 and 2003, and *Catz Galore* for Cat'n Around Downtown. Nelson is a local artist and Johnson is a graduate student at Alverno College. Together with these extraordinary students they enjoy creating art projects for the benefit of the community.

Sponsor: Senator Cathy Stepp

Maiko

. . . a geiko (or geisha) in training.

Artists: Tabitha Krug with Anne Wendland, Shelley Beier and Annika Paulbeck, Milwaukee

All members of this artistic quartet are sophomores at Wisconsin Lutheran College. Krug is an artist and publicist for Vision of Anime Club, Milwaukee, and WLC's dining services. Wendland enjoys exploring different art media, her current interest being sculpture. Paulbeck is most interested in ceramics, sculpture and photography. Beier's favorite subjects are animals and people in nature.

Sponsor: Hartmann Design, Inc.

Polar Beartician

. . . really surrounded by her work.

Artist: Catherine Coe, Racine

Racine native Catherine Coe is a graduate of St. Catherine's High School and a nurse practitioner student at University of Wisconsin-Parkside. She loves to spend time with kids, so she baby-sits for family and friends. Art is a way for her to relax. She enjoys seeing the results of her artistic activities. Creating her bear was a challenge to herself to see what she could accomplish.

Sponsor: Shear Madness

Prize-winning Bears

Bizarro (the Bear)

Northwest Coast Bear

Bean E. Bear

Three judges spent more than four hours in early May determining which bears would win cash prizes – $3,000 for first, $2,000 for second and $1,000 for third – awarded to the artists by Downtown Racine Corporation.

The three judged the bears based on creativity, appeal, workmanship, durability and other criteria, then named their winners: *Bizarro (the Bear)*, created by Jared Joslin of Chicago and sponsored by Knight-Barry Title, Inc., first place; *Northwest Coast Bear*, created by Kristin Gjerdset of Milwaukee and sponsored by Avenue Gallery and Frame, second place; and *Bean E. Bear*, created by Jeff Levonian of Racine and sponsored by Dimples Fine Imports, third place. Winners were announced in June.

About the Judges

All three judges, secured by Lisa Englander, museum store manager at Racine Art Museum, commented on the high quality of the 154 bears. They said the judging was difficult because of the quality and "lots of good stuff." Because of their varied backgrounds and experience, each brought a different perspective to the judging process.

Barbara Brown Lee of New Berlin, Wisconsin, chief educator for the Milwaukee Art Museum, has logged 41 years with the museum, during which she has seen it grow and change considerably. As its chief educator, Brown Lee heads the docent program as well as assists in planning lectures, seminars, school programs and extensive offerings of art appreciation and studio

Judges left to right, JoAnna Poehlmann, Anthony Stoeveken and Barbara Brown Lee review their selections with DRC Executive Director Devin Sutherland.

classes. She also serves as a teacher in the Milwaukee Art Museum-Milwaukee Public Schools high school satellite program and is a frequent lecturer for university classes and community groups. Brown Lee is renowned for her wit and energy and her ability to present art in a way that is meaningful to kids, especially teens, who are her favorite age group.

JoAnna Poehlmann is marking her 50th year as an artist. A Milwaukee native, she is an illustrator and designer of books, greeting cards for Caspari, art for department store ads and fashion houses. She also does gallery work consisting of drawings, prints, collage and limited-edition artists' books. Poehlmann, who studied at Layton School of Art and Marquette University, has been a lecturer at the University of Wisconsin-Milwaukee. She is a recycler of objects and images, something she has done since long before the practice became popular. According to a recent *Milwaukee Journal Sentinel* article, "Poehlmann's artwork draws heavily from nature. She uses animals, insects and plants as her inspiration. Taxidermy animals sit more patiently for

their portraits [in her home] than the wild animals outside…."

Anthony C. Stoeveken, Mequon, Wisconsin, has been professor of art emeritus at the University of Wisconsin-Milwaukee since 1999, following a 28-year career there as professor of art. Prior to joining the UW-M staff in 1970, he spent two years as technical director of GraphicStudio at the University of South Florida in Tampa and three years with Tamarind Lithography Workshop in Los Angeles. His bachelor of science degree in art education and his master of science in fine arts are both from the University of Wisconsin-Milwaukee. During his career he received a wide variety of grants to advance his work, among them from UW-M, the Wisconsin Arts Board and the Ford Foundation.

High Honors

In addition to selecting the top prize winners, the judges named 10 bears for high honors. They are:
After the Reign of Cats and Dogs, created by Bill Reid, sponsored by Sam and Gene Johnson; *Al-beart Einstein*, created by Melissa Rogalla, sponsored by Adecco; *Bare Witness Holmes*, created by Lynn Spleas, sponsored by St. Lucy Catholic Church; *Bear Minimum*, created by Christopher Dembroski, sponsored by E. C. Styberg Engineering Co., Inc.; *Bear-a-Tone*, created by Mary Elizabeth Nelson, sponsored by JobsinRacine.com; *Bearnini Fountain*, created by Darin Weisensel, sponsored by Jazzercise on the Northside; *Bearzan*, created by Brenda Stephan, sponsored by Racine Zoological Society; *Biker Bear*, created by Daniel McConnell, sponsored by Rochelle and Robb Ehrhart; *Polar Beartician*, created by Catherine Coe, sponsored by Shear Madness; and *The Red Baron*, created by Trudi Theisen, sponsored by North Shore Bank.

Honorable Mentions

The judges also cited 20 creations for honorable mention. They are:
Bear in a Blanket, created by Ada James, sponsored by Carpetland, USA; *Bearatone*, created by Barbara Lindquist, sponsored by Sierra Inc.; *Bear-ee-More*, created by Lorna Hennig, sponsored by Tri City National Bank; *Bearie Prairie*, created by Lynn Jones, sponsored by Jay and Ric Ruffo; *China Bear*, created by Sarah Mosk, sponsored by David and Terry Rayburn; *Fat Dominoes on Mr. Blue Berry Hill*, created by Violet O'Dell, sponsored by Sharon Hill, D.C.; *The Great Bearracuda*, created by Krista Lea Meinert Edquist, sponsored by Diamond/Laser Services;

Grin and Bear It, created by Tanya Fuhrman, sponsored by Montfort's Fine Art; *Lilies, Tulips and Bears! Oh My!*, created by Dorothy Smalancke and Amy Kratochvil, sponsored by John and Dianne Palmgren; *Lions and Tigers and Bears, Oh My!*, created by Angela Perrault, sponsored by Nielsen Machine Co., Inc.

Also, *Mardi Grrrras!*, created by Megan Hunt and Heather Johnson, sponsored by N. Christensen and Son; *Old Glory Bear*, created by Lou Ann Urness and Jim Beaugrand, sponsored by Studio 75 Aveda Salon and Day Spa; *Paint by Numbear*, created by Jeani Berndt, sponsored by Econoprint of Racine; *Quilty*, created by Nita Showers, sponsored by Bonnie and Tom Prochaska; *Racine Bumble Bear*, created by Bill Reid, sponsored by Schorsch Management/Green Bay Meadows Apartments; *Rocking Bear*, created by Amy Zahalka, sponsored by Racine Heritage Museum; *Romare Bearden on Our Block*, created by Georgette Hardy Edwards, sponsored by Landmark Title of Racine, Inc.; *Sir Bearlock Holmes*, created by Amy Davis, sponsored by Young Rembrandts-A Children's Drawing Program; *"Sweetness,"* created by Russell Asala and Marsha Sokel, sponsored by Nicholas Industries; and *William Shakesbeare A Midsummer Night's Dream*, created by Theresa Schiffer, sponsored by *Milwaukee Journal Sentinel*.

September Auction

All 154 bears are sold at auction on Saturday afternoon, September 18, at Racine's Memorial Hall. The 33 honored bears are featured in a voice auction while the remainder are sold in a silent auction.

About Downtown Racine Corporation

Mission Statement

The Downtown Racine Corporation will be the leader in the continued economic, aesthetic and recreational revitalization of Downtown and its neighborhoods.

We will be proactive in the retention of existing business. We will facilitate new developments by promoting public/private investments and partnerships, and working cooperatively with the other economic development organizations.

In all that we do, we will communicate effectively with our members, partners, many diversified neighbors and the public at large.

Vision Statement

Downtown Racine will be:

- A symbol of the community's pride.
- A center of celebration and recreation on the lake.
- A harmonious mixture of residential, commercial, cultural, recreational and governmental activities.
- A safe, convenient and aesthetically pleasing place to live, work, shop, visit and play.
- Respectful of its historical character, its charm and waterfront setting.
- Pedestrian and driver-friendly with efficient traffic circulation, signage and convenient and safe parking.
- A unique retail center serving the needs of its neighborhood, the community and visitors.
- People-oriented and neighborhood for all neighbors.

Downtown Racine Corporation Board of Directors

Chairman: Scott Kelly, Johnson Bank
Vice Chairman: Micah Waters, Porters of Racine
Secretary: Joanne Labre, Dover Flag and Map
Treasurer: Bernie Powers, Knuteson, Powers and Wheeler, S.C.
Past President: Brian Anderson, SC Johnson

Government Officials

Gary Becker, Mayor
William McReynolds, County Executive
Cherri Cape, Alderman
Jeff Coe, Alderman

Board

Jim Beck, All Saints Healthcare
John Crimmings, N. Christensen and Son, Inc.
Dave Foster, Design Partners, Inc.
Jerry Franke, WISPARK LLC
Brad Harring, Avenue Gallery and Frame
Mike Jack, CNH Global
Dennis Navratil, Downtown Property Owner
Mary Beth Ormiston, Racine Family YMCA
Kelly Semrau, SC Johnson
Jim Spodick, Historic Century Market
Mike Staeck, Landmark Title of Racine, Inc.
Fiona Zaleski, Downtown Property Owner

Downtown Racine Corporation Staff

Devin Sutherland, Executive Director
Jean Garbo, Marketing Director
Terry Leopold, Special Events Coordinator
Elaina McLain, Accountant
Lennie Farrington, Receptionist

Index of
Artist Profiles

Index of Bear Portraits

Index of Sponsors